Cultural Graphology

Cultural Graphology

Writing after Derrida

JULIET FLEMING

The University of Chicago Press ❁ *Chicago and London*

The University of Chicago Press, Chicago 60637
The University of Chicago Press, Ltd., London

Paperback edition 2018
Printed in the United States of America

27 26 25 24 23 22 21 20 19 18   2 3 4 5 6

ISBN-13: 978-0-226-39042-0 (cloth)
ISBN-13: 978-0-226-56519-4 (paper)
ISBN-13: 978-0-226-39056-7 (e-book)
DOI: https://doi.org/10.7208/chicago/9780226390567.001.0001

Publication costs were supported by the Department of English at New York University, through the generosity of the Abraham and Rebecca Stein Faculty Publication Fund.

Library of Congress Cataloging-in-Publication Data

Names: Fleming, Juliet, author.
Title: Cultural graphology : writing after Derrida / Juliet Fleming.
Description: Chicago ; London : The University of Chicago Press, 2016. | Includes bibliographical references and index.
Identifiers: LCCN 2016001194 | ISBN 9780226390420 (cloth : alk. paper) | ISBN 9780226390567 (e-book)
Subjects: LCSH: Derrida, Jacques. | Literature—History and criticism. | Writing—Social aspects.
Classification: LCC B2430.D484 F55 2016 | DDC 194—dc23
LC record available at http://lccn.loc.gov/2016001194

⊗ This paper meets the requirements of ANSI/NISO Z39.48-1992 (Permanence of Paper).

Contents

Acknowledgments vii

Abbreviations ix

Introduction: From Grammatology to Cultural Graphology *1*

1 The Psychopathology of Writing *31*

2 Type Ornament *51*

3 Sign Tailoring *86*

4 Psychoanalytic Graphology *112*

Notes 143

Index 161

Acknowledgments

I am grateful to the students in Cambridge and New York who lent their youthful energies to reading Derrida with me and to the English translators whose work made that possible. John Forrester, Mary Jacobus, Sarah Kay, and other members of the Cambridge Psychoanalytic Reading Group offered stimulating conversation as I started work on this project, and the department of English at NYU, and the wider community of scholars in New York City and New Haven, provided a congenial environment in which to finish it. Jason Scott-Warren and Adam Smyth have been generous friends, interlocutors, and guides to the archive. Two anonymous reports (in one of which I recognized the brilliant hand of Tom Conley) and the careful scrutiny of Gary Tomlinson and Margreta de Grazia allowed me to significantly improve the final manuscript. I am indebted to all four readers for their transformative suggestions and corrections. Margreta has for many years cast her protective brilliance over the slow growth of this book. My deepest thanks are to her; to my son Raymond Fleming, who followed his mother up the steep paths of his childhood without flagging or complaint, until it became my turn to follow him; and to my dearest husband and partner in thought, Gary Tomlinson, to whom this book is dedicated.

Abbreviations

Works by Derrida

AC	"Aphorism Countertime." Translated by Nicholas Royle. In *Acts of Literature*, edited by Derek Attridge, 414–33. London and New York: Routledge, 1992.
AF	*Archive Fever: A Freudian Impression*. Translated by Eric Prenowitz. Chicago: University of Chicago Press, 1996.
C	"Circumfession." Translated by Geoffrey Bennington. In *Jacques Derrida* (in collaboration with Geoffrey Bennington). Chicago: University of Chicago Press, 1993.
CC	"Che cos'è la poesia?" Translated by Peggy Kamuf. In *A Derrida Reader: Between the Blinds*, edited by Peggy Kamuf, 221–37. London: Harvester, 1991.
D	*Dissemination*. Translated by Barbara Johnson. Chicago: University of Chicago Press, 1981.
DN	*Deconstruction in a Nutshell: A Conversation with Jacques Derrida*. Edited by John C. Caputo. New York: Fordham University Press, 1995.

E	*The Ear of the Other: Otobiography, Transference, Translation*. Edited by Christie McDonald and translated by Peggy Kamuf. Lincoln: University of Nebraska Press, 1988.
ED	*L'écriture et la différence*. Paris, Éditions du Seuil, 1967.
F	"Fors: The Anglish Words of Nicolas Abrahms and Maria Torok." Translated by Barbara Johnson. Foreword to *The Wolf Man's Magic Word*, by Nicholas Abraham and Maria Torok, xi–xlviii. Minneapolis: University of Minnesota Press.
G	*Glas*. Translated by John P. Leavey Jr. and Richard Rand. Lincoln: University of Nebraska Press, 1990.
GD	*The Gift of Death*. Translated by David Wills. Chicago: University of Chicago Press, 1995.
Grammatology	*Of Grammatology*. Translated by Gayatri Spivak. Baltimore: Johns Hopkins University Press, 1976.
HE	"Heidegger's Ear: Philopolemology (Geschlecht IV)." Translated by John Leavey Jr. In *Reading Heidegger: Commemorations*, edited by John Sallis, 163–218. Bloomington: Indiana University Press, 1992.
ITS	"I Have a Taste for the Secret." In *A Taste for the Secret*, by Jacques Derrida and Maurizio Ferraris. Translated by Giacomo Donis and edited by Giacomo Donis and David Webb. Cambridge: Polity Press, 2001.
M	"Mallarmé." Translated by Christine Roulston. In *Acts of Literature*, edited by Derek Attridge, 110–25. London: Routledge, 1992.
MC	"Mes Chances: A Rendezvous with Some Epicurean Stereophonies." Translated by Irene Harvey and Avital Ronnell. In *Taking Chances:*

	Derrida, Psychoanalysis and Literature, edited by H. Smith and W. Kerrigan, 1–32. Baltimore: Johns Hopkins University Press, 1984.
MP	*Margins of Philosophy*. Translated by Alan Bass. Chicago: University of Chicago Press, 1982.
MS	"Maddening the Subjectile." Translated by Mary Ann Caws. *Yale French Studies* 84 (1984): 154–71.
OT	*On Touching—Jean-Luc Nancy*. Translated by Christine Irizarry. Stanford: Stanford University Press, 2005.
PC	*The Postcard*. Translated by Alan Bass. Chicago: University of Chicago Press, 1987.
PM	*Paper Machine*. Translated by Rachel Bowlby. Stanford, CA: Stanford University Press, 2005.
Po	*Positions*. Translated by Alan Bass. Chicago: University of Chicago Press, 1981.
Pt	*Points . . . Interviews 1974–1994*. Edited by Elisabeth Weber and translated by Peggy Kamuf et al. Stanford, CA: Stanford University Press, 1995.
PT	"The Purveyor of Truth." Translated by Willis Domingo, James Hubert, Moshe Ron, and M.–R. L. *Yale French Studies* 52 (1975): 31–113.
PTT	"Punctuations: The Time of a Thesis." Translated by Kathleen McLaughlin. In *Philosophy in France Today*, edited by A. Montefiore, 34–50. Cambridge: Cambridge University Press, 1983.
R	*Resistances of Psychoanalysis*. Translated by Peggy Kamuf, Pascale-Anne Brault, and Michael Naas. Stanford, CA: Stanford University Press, 1998.
Sc	"Scribble (Writing Power)." *Yale French Studies* 58 (1979): 117–47.
SI	"'This Strange Institution Called Literature': An Interview with Jacques Derrida." In *Acts*

	of Literature, edited by Derek Attridge, 33–75. London: Routledge, 1992.
TP	*The Truth in Painting*. Translated by Geoff Bennington and Ian McLeod. Chicago: University of Chicago Press, 1987.
VP	*Voice and Phenomenon: Introduction to the Problem of the Sign in Husserl's Phenomenology*. Translated by Leonard Lawlor. Evanston, IL: Northwestern University Press, 2011.
WD	*Writing and Difference*. Translated by Alan Bass. Chicago: University of Chicago Press, 1978.
WRT	"What Is a 'Relevant' Translation?" Translated by Lawrence Venuti. *Critical Inquiry* 27, no. 2 (Winter 2001): 174–200.

Other Works

CJ	Kant, Immanuel. *Kant's Critique of Aesthetic Judgement*. Translated by James Creed Meredith. Oxford: Clarendon Press, 1911.
Écrits	Lacan, Jacques. *Écrits: A Selection*. Translated by Alan Sheridan. London: Tavistock, 1977.
LGR	Klein, Melanie. *Love, Guilt and Reparation and Other Works, 1921–1945*. London: Vintage, 1998.
SE	Freud, Sigmund. *The Standard Edition of the Complete Psychological Works of Sigmund Freud*. Translated by James Strachey, in collaboration with Anna Freud, assisted by Alix Strachey and Alan Tyson. 24 vols. London: Hogarth, 1953–74.
SPL	Lacan, Jacques. "The Seminar of the Purloined Letter." Translated by Jeffrey Mehlman. *Yale French Studies* 48 (1973): 39–72.

Introduction

From Grammatology to Cultural Graphology

Analytical bibliography: the study of books as physical objects; the details of their production, the effects of the method of manufacture on the text. When Sir Walter Greg called bibliography a science of the transmission of literary documents, he was referring to analytical bibliography. Analytical bibliography may deal with the history of printers and booksellers, with the description of paper or bindings, or with textual matters arising during the progression from writer's manuscript to published book.
«TERRY BELANGER[1]»

Of Grammatology is the title of a question: a question about the necessity of a science of writing, about the conditions that would make it possible, about the critical work that would have to open its field and resolve the epistemological obstacles; but it is also a question about the limits of this science
«DERRIDA, *Positions*, 13»

Cultural graphology names a new approach to the study of texts; it is the work of this book to explore and explain it. But I have hesitated over my subtitle. I first thought to identify the field that was to be changed by Derrida's thought as *bibliography*, which is, strictly speaking, the study of the material transmission of texts. But since cultural graphology is a speculative and interpretative discipline with a much wider task than that of bibliography, and since I have no practical commitment to bibliography, *Book History after Derrida* seemed a better description of what I am up to. And yet this project cannot be described as book history, nor can it even be described as the transformation of that field. First, because I have scarcely engaged with the work of even the most eminent book historians, second, and more consequentially, because I take seriously Derrida's observation that both the Greek term "*biblos*" and its Latin counterpart "*liber*" first designated not books but rather the papery support for writing that was derived from plant material (*PM* 6). My readings thus resist many of the assumptions on which book history is built. Indeed, my topic, as I have come to recognize and name it, is *writing conceived without the guardrails of the book*.

I should also acknowledge that my use of literary theory is also both selective and motivated. Although I am old enough to have met Derrida or at least to have heard him speak, I did neither. I am not part of that group of Derrida's friends and colleagues who, in writing about him now, must continue to mourn his passing, nor do I seek to position my work among theirs. If many excellent readers of Derrida are not mentioned or are mentioned too briefly in what follows, this is because I do not seek to intervene in Derrida's legacy in any programmatic way. Rather, my aim is to use his writing in tandem with what is currently being done in book history to throw light on the local initiative that Derrida tentatively called *cultural graphology*. While I hope the result proves to be theoretically suggestive, I am primarily writing for those interested in the history of texts who want to do something other than what they could do just as well (or better) as bibliographers, philologists, or historians of reading. It is for such readers that I am propounding whatever of Derrida's thought might be most useful for their own purposes.[2] And if, by the end of this, you are exhausted, it is certain that, as Derrida said of his own reading of Genet, "you will not have exhausted" the resources of Derrida's writing (*G* 117b).

Still, it must be admitted that the personal stimulus for this project is my long engagement with, and desire to do justice to,

Derrida's mistranslated, overpraised, and undervalued magnum opus *De la Grammatologie* (1967), a work already old when I was young. I will begin by explaining the grip it has exerted on me over many years.

We must start with a bibliographical issue, a warning in Derrida's own words: "in what you call my books, what is first of all put into question is the unity of the book and the unity 'book' . . . with all the implications of such a concept" (*Po* 3). Derrida defies the borders and boundaries of what we normally call a book by playing with typographic conventions, asserting that he has not yet begun when he gets to the end of a work, or by writing several volumes at once, fracturing, blending, and redistributing arguments within and between them. His early work was often provoked by readings of other writers that were so close, so parasitic, that the inexperienced can find it hard to distinguish Derrida's commentary from what it is commenting on—and here the question of where a book begins and ends is already pressing. Derrida also used his own writing as the occasion for further thought, and would have been the first to say that he was never *done with* anything; he was preoccupied with the proposition that if nothing is ever simply there as its present self, nor is it ever simply gone (this is what he means by "*différance*"). And as if all this were not already enough to baffle a bibliographer, to read Derrida's writing is to experience that "presentiment" that Jean-Luc Nancy described in relation to Derrida's work as the sensation that "allows us to already know that which has nevertheless not yet begun."[3] You can scarcely see three paces in front of you, you can't begin to say what might happen, and yet you are feeling that it has already occurred and is only awaiting the confirmation of your reading eye.

Although another of Derrida's famous neologisms "*destinerrance*" is designed to *avoid* the thought that anything runs a determined course (he once said, in response to a question as to where he was going with an argument, "I'll say that I'm trying to get to the point where I myself don't know where I'm going") he was, nevertheless, the conscious architect of presentiment as a sensation and sensitive to his own experience of it when reading the work of others—writing on Jean-Luc Nancy, he confessed in turn, "I've hardly taken a step and he's already running ahead of me, never out of breath, touching and re-touching his text, taxing my belatedness in advance" (*OT* 131).[4] This vision of Derrida outstripped by his prolific friend will comfort and amuse his own readers (you should know that no one has ever come close to keeping up with Derrida—no serious reader should try). But it is not only Nancy's continuing output that forces Derrida to fall behind, like Tristram Shandy narrating his own life and finding after six weeks of hard writing that he has not yet got to the moment of his birth; rather, it is Derrida's own sense that whatever he can find to say about Nancy's writing has already been anticipated by that writing.[5] Put so bluntly, this may describe the position of any literary critic, but as I know from my own reading of Derrida, presentiment is something other than this: it is the experience of being bound and freed by a powerful text. So in his account of the *Phaedrus* in *Dissemination* (1972), after a long digression on the relation of myths to philosophical discourse, Derrida advises readers that he will now return to Plato's text, "assuming we have ever really left it" (*D* 98). He made the same gesture in "Mes Chances" (1983) to indicate that at some level, whatever else he is doing, he is never not reading Freud, and ten years later he was still not done, remarking that years of such reading had done nothing to assuage his engagement with Freud's themes, "with figures, with conceptual schemes that are familiar to me to the point of obsession and yet remain no less secret, young and still to come" (*AF* 26).

In "Aphorism Countertime," a reading of *Romeo and Juliet*, Derrida developed the concept of presentiment as a theme not only of that play but of drama itself: We hope everything will turn out well, we believe that it might, and yet, even before the curtain goes up, even before the lovers are coupled together, we know from the names Romeo and Juliet that disaster has already struck (*AC* 414–33). In a comedy, similarly, we know that mischance is inevitable, even if we can't predict the form it will take. Still, presentiment is more than a theory of drama, and even to call it the single theme of literature would be to straiten it, for it is the burden and mood of writing itself, a name for its propensity to look forward as well as back: "it is because writing is inaugural, in the primal sense of the word, that it is dangerous and anguishing. It does not know where it is going, no knowledge can keep it from the essential precipitation towards the meaning that it constitutes, and that is, primarily, its future" (*WD* 11).

Which is another way of saying that, with or without us, ready or not, writing is what happens. Or even better, since writing, like everything else, is constitutively out of joint and can never be punctual to its own occasion, we might say that writing is what *just happened*. Derrida gave testimony that this was his own experience as an author when in 1983 he told an interviewer who had incautiously asked about his "destiny" as a writer that what he wrote "resembles a dotted-line drawing that would be circling around a book to be written in what I call for myself 'the old new language,' the most archaic and the most novel, therefore unheard-of, unreadable at present. This book would be . . . an interminable anamnesis whose form is being sought." "Are you going to write it?" she persisted. "You must be joking," he replied (*Pt* 119). The uncanny feeling that things are precipitating without intention towards an unknown future that both could and could not have been different is, I think, a fundamental literary effect, and one that is intimately linked to what Derrida calls the literality of the letter. I explore these issues in later chapters. For now we need only note presentiment as one factor among others that should deter those who seek answers to old fashioned bibliographical questions about Derrida's work.

Had you also persisted (for after all, didn't he devote almost twenty-five pages of *Grammatology* to the question of the chronology of Rousseau's writings?), had you asked Derrida, as one who ought to know, *what* of his work was written *when*, you should not have expected a straight answer, and you might have been treated to something like this:

> *Of Grammatology* can be taken as a long essay divided into two parts, between which one can stitch in *Writing and Difference*. The *Grammatology* often refers to this work. In which case the interpretation of Rousseau would be the twelfth essay [actually the thirteenth] in that collection. Conversely, one can insert *Of Grammatology* in the middle of *Writing and Difference*. While six essays of the latter are anterior, in fact and in principle, to the publication . . . of the articles announcing *Of Grammatology*, the last five, beginning with "Freud and the Scene of Writing" are engaged in the grammatological opening. (*Po* 12–13, translation modified)

Here Derrida is not just saying that *Grammatology* and *Writing and Difference* each contain the other within themselves or that the two volumes were written simultaneously or in relay both with each other and with *Voice and Phenomenon* (the third volume he published in 1967) or that, as he argued more than once, "not one of them was a book," although each of these claims is sufficiently striking.[6] He is also reminding us that within any book there are many books and that within *Grammatology* you can find the groundwork for several works that could have been and could still be differently built. (To take Derrida very seriously on this point would be to allow the possibility that books that have *already* been written, perhaps books written centuries before he was born, are versions of the *Grammatology* to come, but I am not going to pursue that here.)

You could certainly say that much of what Derrida wrote after 1967 was his way of realizing these projects. He later came to feel that *Grammatology* was the seedbed of his intellectual career, and you can see why. It is there that he famously argued that, since a text's context, out of which its meaning is produced, must be adduced but can never be fully delimited or described, there is nothing outside or irrelevant to that text ("*Il n'y a pas d'hors-texte*") (*Grammatology* 158). And it is within *Grammatology* that he began to present the insights that he there called *différance*, *the trace*, and *the supplement*, while demonstrating his own piercing reading practice, his way of stepping through canonical works with a dramatically heightened caution that refused to accept either the anxieties or the consolations of philosophy as these have commonly been used to establish the meaning of texts. Readers have loved *Grammatology* for the same reason they have hated it—because it works "to make enigmatic what one thinks one understands" (*Grammatology* 70).

So in her dazzling and influential introduction to the English translation of *Grammatology* (1974), Gayatri Spivak positioned Derrida as the theorist of différance and as the engineer of a reading method that was shortly to become codified and known as *deconstruction*. For the young Spivak, and for the many readers who have found her introduction easier to grasp than Derrida's text, grammatology was deconstruction as it questions the philosophical concepts we assume when making sense of things: it is "the science of the *sous rature*," of the "effacement of the trace." The visual gimmick of sous rature is designed to suggest that, since our analyses can do neither with nor without these traditional concepts, we should use them as Heidegger did—"under erasure." But if for both thinkers sous rature reminds us that definitions of truth and meaning "must be established on assertions in which thinking dies out," deconstruction attempts to establish, not (as Heidegger might) the unthinkable within those assertions but rather the fact that they are unthinkable (*Grammatology* xiii–xx).

In his early career Derrida threw out a series of terms that gave local habitations to the general proposition that we cannot think the foundations of meaning: *Grammatology* has not only "sous rature" (used of an unsatisfactory term which we must still employ) but also "trace" (to suggest that what a signifier marks is not only "not there" but, more importantly, "not that": the trace is not the remainder of something gone but the mark of what was never fully there); "the supplement" (which completes an entity and thereby shows it never was or could be entire in and of itself); "différance" (to indicate that meaning is both delayed and not itself except by being produced out of differences); "spacing" (the proposition that life is essentially divided against itself since it is lived both in time and in relation to things outside itself);

and "*entamer*" (to begin not at the beginning, which we can't find, but where we are, "with a trace, without initiating anything" [*TP* 11]). Still, the term that dominates and organizes *Grammatology*, both as its theoretical insight and as its special preoccupation, is "writing."

Now, grammatology means "the law or science or speech (*logos*) of writing (*gramme*)." Derrida's title thus keeps alive the sense of a struggle between speech and writing (each jostling to get the law on its side) as well as the thought that these may, after all, prove impossible to distinguish (the fact that *speech gets no closer than writing to being able to manifest presence* is a point on which Derrida insists). The French title, *De la grammatologie*, suggests a discourse *about* grammatology that yet comes *from* it—Spivak could have translated the title as *Towards*, *From*, *About*, *On*, or even *Some Grammatology*. And, like *Of Grammatology*, each of these translations would suggest that we are dealing with a discourse or discipline that is not yet fully present, not fully accounted for, or—to use a term the interest of which fully occurred to Derrida only later in his career—not fully *supported*. Since grammatology is thus already the question of its own possibility, I have chosen to depart from Spivak's practice by dropping Derrida's prefix when translating his title into English and simply calling it *Grammatology*.

Within *Grammatology* the term "writing" comes to mean not just graphic notation, which Derrida distinguishes as "writing in the narrow sense," but every technique of designation—including those of the voice. But it doesn't stop there, for by writing Derrida also means the trace-structure in general or différance itself as it inhabits all things and experiences in the world. This is perhaps most easily explained by saying that for Derrida a thing never exists *as such* but always and only in its relation to and difference from other things. Signification occurs where there are differences, and these differences are all that is required for there to be writing. Writing in this enlarged sense not only has no necessary connection to what we normally mean by inscription, but it is *not yet semiotic*—it is better thought of as *information*, as that may be said to exist before (and in much greater quantities than) meaning.[7] Indeed, if we understand writing as the occurrence of difference before it is read or noted by a third party, we could deepen the claim that something about writing is best described as *what happens* and say instead that there is something about writing that has always already happened (you may have had a presentiment that I was going to argue this!).

In the opening chapters of *Grammatology* Derrida calls this trace-structure *arche-writing*, which usefully suggests that the trace-structure, or lack of origin, is at the base of all things. In later chapters, however, he simply uses the term "writing" on its own, which has the advantage of helping us discern that there can be no clear point of demarcation between writing in the narrow sense and arche-writing. Already you can see how this proposition both supports and redirects the work of those textual scholars who aim to establish texts within the contexts of their production and consumption and who are increasingly learning to include labor, technology, performance, transmission, bodies, locations, and institutions among these contexts.

Of course, you can also see here just how Derrida's thinking goes far beyond what it is necessary, or even useful, for historians of the book to retain. My aim is to put on the table those of Derrida's thoughts and gestures that best shake up bibliographical confidence. When the dust settles I expect that science to proceed as usual, but perhaps it will find itself, without knowing why, and without reading Derrida, able to ask new questions about itself and its objects.

With the exception of its introduction and an important chapter "Of Grammatology as a Positive Science," *Grammatology* then comprises close readings of texts by Saussure, Levi-Strauss, and—at much greater length—Rousseau. Derrida attends to these figures because they each position writing as the villain of the piece, as if each one of them had, at some level, recognized that the human voice is compromised as the register of presence, and each time used writing (whose case appears to be worse) to deny what they knew. As Derrida sees it, it is because writing is so often used as a scapegoat for the unacknowledged shortcomings of speech that it serves as the obvious place in which to begin an investigation into philosophy's motivated ignorance of the trace in general.

And yet, as Spivak felt and remarked, Derrida's commitment to the topic of writing seems to have further determinants, as if writing was drawing attention to itself as something other than a special case of the trace. Arguing that writing does not remain an important conceptual master-word for Derrida after *Grammatology*, Spivak suggested that his decision to use it here is polemical, aimed perhaps "against the manifest phonocentrism of structuralism" (as it certainly is) (*Grammatology* lxix). She notes further that Part I of *Grammatology* is an expansion of a very long, two-part review article Derrida had just written about three books which were all deeply concerned with writing (Madeleine V. David's *Le débat sur les écritures et l'hiéroglyphe aux XVII et XVIII siècles*, André Leroi-Gourhan's *Gesture and Speech*, and papers from a colloquium collected by Marcel Cohen titled *L'écriture et la psychologie des peuples*).[8] "One cannot help wondering," Spivak concludes,

> if all this overt interest in an account of writing in the narrow sense—rather than in the interpretation of texts—is not simply due to the regulating presence of books to be reviewed. Indeed, in Part I and in the postscript to "Freud and the Scene of Writing," Derrida speaks most often of re-writing the "history of writing" in something suspiciously like the narrow sense—"an immense field where hitherto one has only done preparatory work" (*ED* 340). "Writing" so envisaged is on the brink of becoming a unique signifier, and Jacques Derrida's chief care. In his later work, the theoretical significance of the structure of writing and the grammatological opening remain intact. But he quietly drops the idea of being the authorized grammatological historian of writing in the narrow sense. "Writing" then takes its place on the chain of substitutions [of conceptual master-terms].

"In the *Grammatology*, then," Spivak concludes, "we are at a specific and precarious moment in Derrida's career," when he looked as if he might become a mere "grammarian" (*Grammatology* lxxix–lxxx).

Few read Spivak's introduction to *Grammatology* without being helped by her understanding of the work—a grasp all the more impressive given its early date in the reception of Derrida's writing. To date no one has attempted a comparable analysis of the work, and while a more accurate translation of it is still overdue, a better introduction to this strange, multiply functioned, and many-voiced book might never be written.[9] But although Spivak anticipated that "the theoretical significance" of what she calls "the structure of writing" would remain intact in Derrida's future work, we can now see that she and others after her signally underestimated the nature and the consequence of Derrid commitment to the question of writing both within and beyond *Grammatology*. In fact, ten years after its first appearance, at the moment when Spivak was arguing that Derrida had moved on from the topic of writing in the narrow sense, he was working on an essay whose title and subtitle demonstrate his ongoing commitment to a topic whose specificity would continue to vivify and punctuate his life's work—namely, "Scribble (writing power): Who Can Write? What Can Writing Do?"[10]

In truth, there can be no serious doubt that Derrida was and remained a grammarian—that is, a scholar concerned with the techniques of gathering, ordering, and transmitting knowledge. Since these concerns are intimately bound to questions of writing, we should perhaps say that all scholars of literature and the other lettered arts (not to mention all scholars of the digital humanities) are grammarians. But among this group Derrida is more of a grammarian than most, a grammarian *in the narrow sense*, for he continued throughout his life to discover local topics about writing that he could position as a platform for the entirety of his concerns. Asked in 2001 about his relation to electronic media, he said that the question gave him the impression ("impression! what a word, already!") that he had never had any other subject than paper: "I have always written, and even spoken, on paper: on the subject of paper, on actual paper, and with paper in mind." (By then his engagement with the term *impression* had also been a long one, and in 1995 he had used it to organize his account of Freud's legacy in *Archive Fever*.) Furthermore, if the themes of "support, subject, surface, mark, trace, written mark, inscription, fold" had always, he said, exerted a tenacious grip on him, by 2001 he had come to feel that his obsession had been "increasingly justified and confirmed" by the fact that the technological hegemony of paper was coming to an end in a period that roughly coincided with the length of his own lifetime (*PM* 41). The title of the interview, "Paper or Me," suggests not only that the paper form was facing a repurposed and remediated survival but also that Derrida understood his thought to be perishable and inextricably bound to the particular technologies of paper that had made it possible.

Spivak's celebration of what she saw as Derrida's turn away from writing in the narrow sense certainly yielded results. Plucking the motifs of deconstruction from the tangled cloth of *Grammatology*, and discarding the topic of writing while retaining philosophy as the background to the new method, she laid the ground for what was soon to emerge as the Yale school of deconstruction. But the first casualty of this development was *Grammatology* itself, quickly displaced (except among his detractors) as Derrida's masterpiece, and now too often passed over.

But perhaps it is Derrida himself who should be blamed for this. In the *exergue* that serves as preface to the book, and so has some claim to be the last as well as the first word on the matter, Derrida warned his readers that it would not be easy to be a grammatologist, not least because it would be hard to describe what you were doing: "I would like to suggest above all that . . . such a science of writing runs the risk of never being established as such and with that name. Of never being able to define the unity of its project or its object. Of not being able either to write its discourse on method or to describe the limits of its field" (*Grammatology* 4). Spivak's sense that, after *Grammatology*, the topic of writing might be considered closed is supported within the text, for in 1967 Derrida conceived the problem of writing as being "at the root of all sciences," at once too vast and too transcendent to be dealt with as if it were a question of local or even global history. Grammatology could not be merely one among the human sciences; rather, it would be *the* science of man, and beyond that (for the study of man is, after all, only a local study) the science of science (which would also make it the philosophy of philosophy). "On what conditions is a grammatology possible?" Derrida asked himself. "Its fundamental condition is certainly the undoing of logocentrism. But this condition of possibility is also a condition of impossibility. In fact it risks destroying the concept of science as well" (*Grammatology* 74, translation modified).

The daunting nature of the enterprise, and the variety and difficulty of the terrain that would have to be crossed and recrossed within and between the older disciplines in order to give birth to the new, was enough to give even Derrida pause. And there is a specific moment in *Grammatology* where he seems to decline the task, reiterating the fact that, beyond its enormity, grammatology must shatter the assumptions and protocols of science and philosophy and so cut away the very places where its problems might be grasped:

> The meta-rationality or the meta-scientificity which are thus announced within the meditation upon writing can therefore be no more shut up within a science of man than conform to the traditional idea of science. In one and the same gesture, they leave *man, science,* and the *line* behind. (*Grammatology* 87)[11]

But at this moment a strange thing happens, as Derrida pauses in order to dismiss a still less satisfactory way of doing grammatology: "even less can this meditation be contained within the limits of a regional science." The formulation is, as the English used to say, a regular facer, it stops you in your tracks. *Why* can't grammatology be a regional science? Isn't it precisely those sciences that can't be founded as such that most benefit from the multidisciplinary and local approaches of regional study? And didn't Derrida himself conclude in his contemporary discussion of Levi-Strauss's method that there *is* no perfect science—that every discipline has to make do with tools borrowed rather than designed for the job (*WD* 285)? Surely grammatology might very well seek its place as a regional science, adapting the concepts at hand to produce a series of local readings in the history and practice of writing. Derrida's foreclosure of the possibility seems to be a classic case of negation. "What do you think was furthest from your mind at that minute?" Freud asked patients who continued to withhold their repressed unconscious thoughts, "What would you consider the most unlikely imaginable thing in that situation?" Those who fell for the trick almost always revealed the information he sought.[12]

Derrida needed no such prompt. Having said that grammatology could certainly not be a regional science he seems to have been struck by the thought that perhaps it could. "Were it a graphology," he mused, "and even a graphology renewed and fertilized by sociology, history, ethnography, and psychoanalysis. . . ." (*Grammatology* 87). Still, the strange conditional that reigns over the birth of cultural graphology registers its author's lingering resistance, his judgment that, however thoughtfully undertaken, both the general and regional study of grammatology would be ill advised. It was a judgment he reiterated in later years. In 1990 Derrida insisted (perhaps too much) that he had never proposed some positive science or discipline of grammatology but had on the contrary gone "to great lengths to demonstrate the impossibility, the conditions of impossibility, the absurdity, in principle, of any science or philosophy bearing the name 'grammatology'" (*R* 52). But in 1967, when the question was still fresh with him, he went on first to give the impossible local science a name, *cultural graphology*, and then to sketch a blueprint for its pursuit, noting that, before it could speculate on what local writing styles and practices might tell us about ethnographic and other local groups, the new field would have to attend to more "general and fundamental problems" such as Hjelmslev had raised under the rubric of "*graphematics*"—including those

> of the diverse forms of graphic substances (materials: wood, wax, skin, stone, ink, metal, vegetable) or instruments (point, brush etc., etc.); as to the articulation of the technical, economic, or historical levels (for example, at the moment when a graphic *system* is constituted and at the moment, which is not necessarily the same, when a graphic *style*

> is fixed); as to the limit and the sense of variations in style within the system; as to all the investitures to which a *graphie*, in form and substance, is submitted. (*Grammatology* 87)

The exergue to *Grammatology* gives eloquent justification for this slow method of thinking about writing by adducing its unforeseeable future consequences:

> Perhaps patient meditation and painstaking investigation on and around what is still provisionally called writing, far from falling short of a science of writing or hastily dismissing it by some obscurantist reaction, letting it rather develop its positivity as far as possible, are the wanderings of a way of thinking that is faithful and attentive to the ineluctable world of the future which proclaims itself at present, beyond the barriers of knowledge. (*Grammatology* 4, translation modified)

That is, new work on the old topic of writing may open the future of humanistic and scientific thought. And in the simultaneously written "Freud and the Scene of Writing," an essay included in *Writing and Difference*, where it is identified as the first to be "engaged with the grammatological opening," Derrida restated his brief for cultural graphology, and here he sounded almost sanguine about its chances:

> Such a radicalization of the thought of the trace . . . would be fruitful, not only in the deconstruction of logocentrism, but in a kind of reflection exercised more positively, in different fields, at different levels of writing in general, at the point of articulation of writing in the current sense and of the trace in general. These fields, whose specificity thereby could be opened to a thought fecundated by psychoanalysis, would be numerous. (*WD* 230)

At once local and general, attentive to the materials, forms, practices, and institutions of writing in the narrow sense and to the limitations of the ways in which each of these is conceived even as we attempt to account for them, cultural graphology might take hold of itself as a new science by thinking about différance (here described as "the radicalization of the thought of the trace") at those local sites where common sense and the academic disciplines had already tried and failed to account for writing. More simply put (and put in terms that Derrida would not have used), we can use the resources of deconstruction to shake up and enlarge the field that, for the time being, and in spite of its obvious limitations, might still be called *book history*.

Derrida went so far as to indicate four areas where such work might begin—such is the blueprint that he left us (*WD* 230–31):

1. A *psychopathology of everyday life* in which the study of writing would not be limited to the interpretation of the *lapsus calami*, and, moreover, would be more attentive to this latter and to its originality than Freud himself ever was. "*Slips of the pen*, to which I now pass, are so closely akin to slips of the tongue that we have nothing new to expect from them" (*SE* 15:69). This did not prevent Freud from raising the fundamental juridical problem of responsibility, before the tribunal of psychoanalysis, as concerns, for example, the murderous *lapsus calami* (ibid).
2. A *history of writing*, an immense field in which only preparatory work has been done up to now; however admirable this work has been, it still gives way, beyond its empirical discoveries, to unbridled speculation.
3. A *becoming-literary of the literal*. Here, despite several attempts made by Freud and certain of his successors, a psychoanalysis of literature respectful of the *originality of the literary signifier* has not yet begun, and this is surely not an accident. Until now, only the analysis of literary *signifieds*, that is, *non-literary* signified meanings, has been undertaken. But such questions refer to the entire history of literary forms themselves, and to the history of everything within them which was destined precisely to authorize this disdain of the signifier.
4. Finally, to continue designating these fields according to traditional and problematic boundaries, what might be called a new *psychoanalytic graphology*, which would take into account the contributions of the three kinds of research we have just outlined roughly. Here, Melanie Klein perhaps opens the way. As concerns the forms of signs, even within phonetic writing, the cathexes of gestures, and of movements, of letters, lines, points, the elements

> of the writing apparatus (instruments, surface, substance, etc.), a text like *The Role of the School in the Libidinal Development of the Child* (1923) indicates the direction to be taken.
>
> Melanie Klein's entire thematic, her analysis of the constitution of good and bad objects, her genealogy of morals could doubtless begin to illuminate, if followed prudently, the entire problem of the archi-trace, not in its essence (it does not have one), but in terms of valuation and devaluation. Writing as sweet nourishment or as excrement, the trace as seed or mortal germ, wealth or weapon, detritus and/or penis, etc.
>
> How, for example, on the stage of history, can writing as excrement separated from the living body and the sacred flesh of the hieroglyph (Artaud) be put into communication with what is said in *Numbers* about the parched woman drinking the inky dust of the law; or what is said in Ezekiel about the son of man who fills his entrails with the scroll of the law which has become as sweet as honey in his mouth?

But having said so much, Derrida fell silent. He did not pursue the grammatological project by name, and he wrote no more about establishing cultural graphology as its local science. Several explanations could be offered for this. You could say that Derrida's febrile intelligence constantly produced and shed new projects—after all, his writing is full of more that could be said, thoughts there is no time to pursue, essays that will not now be written. Or you might suggest, rather differently, that in fact Derrida *did* pursue the work of grammatology after 1967, just using different terms, either because he had come to feel that his aim could be better realized in this way or because he had simply forgotten this early plan. In works such as *Glas*, *The Truth in Painting*, *The Postcard*, *Archive Fever*, and *Paper Machine* it is easy to recognize the local commitments of what, had Derrida pursued it, we would all now be calling cultural graphology. Or you could argue that since his taste was essentially critical and oriented, at least in the earlier part of his career, to a close reading of texts, Derrida had no interest in working to establish what, had it been possible, must have amounted to an ambitious interdisciplinary program, with all the uncertainties (not to mention the crude certainties) that this involved.

Whatever Derrida's reasons for walking away from the project of cultural graphology (and however lightly conceived his plan for it might have been), in the two decades in which I have been teaching and thinking about *Grammatology* I have found myself wondering if the seam he abandoned did not contain enough riches to reward further exploration. And for the past few years I have been deliberately following the outline of this ghost discipline, engaging topics in literature, psychoanalysis, and the history of writing in order to discover the consequences of recombining them under the single aegis of cultural graphology. This book is the result. It does not pretend to be a sequel to or a full explanation of *Grammatology*; and although I hope it does show how some of the governing assumptions of bibliography might be reconfigured in the wake of Derrida's thought, it should not be regarded as an "application" of his work. Perhaps it is best described using the old fashioned title word "gleanings," as that describes the process of gathering fragments dropped from another writer's harvest, some of which may have been deliberately, perhaps even charitably, left behind.

Gleaning (*glanant*) is a concept for which Derrida himself had use (*G* 18b, 46b, 106b, 198b). It is a recurrent motif in *Glas*, whose left hand column begins "what, after all, of the remain(s), today, for us, here, now, of a Hegel?" while the right cites the accidents and deliberate divisions that have befallen a text by Genet (*G* 1a and 1b). But Derrida's interest in remnants and remains, on what gets left behind or passed over, became ever more pressing and linked to more overtly ethical concerns. In his unpublished seminar of 1990–91, "The Rhetoric of Cannibalism," where, turning back to Klein's work, and to the very passage from Ezekiel with which, in 1967, he closed the blueprint for cultural graphology, he noted that there will always be "leftovers and scraps" from the processes of assimilation and incorporation, always something to be gleaned by and for the future.[13]

Gleaning is, of course, a common metaphor for reading; and Heidegger used it to model the collection or gathering of thought at stake in reading:

> *Lego*, *legein*, Latin *legere*, is the same word as our *lesen* [to collect]: gleaning, collecting wood, harvesting grapes, making a selection, "reading [lesen] a book" is just a variant of "gathering" in the authentic sense [*"ein Buch lesen" is nu rein Abort des "Lesens" in eigentlichen Sinne.*] This means laying one thing next to another, bringing them together as one [*in eines Zusammenbringen*]—in short, gathering [*Sammeln*]; but at the same time, the one is contrasted to the other.[14]

But Heidegger's formulation bleaches out the specificity of gleaning as a practice with biblical sanction that survived in the farmlands of Europe until well into the twentieth century: "And when ye reap the harvest of your land, thou shalt not make clean riddance of the corners of the field when thou reapest, neither shalt thou gather any gleaning of thy harvest: thou shalt leave them unto the poor and to the stranger" (Lev. 23:22).[15] Everybody gathers but only the poor stoop to glean; it is properly the work not of the farmer who brings in the harvest but of those who will not otherwise eat; it is never done from the position of someone who can put their resources in order, for even if the scraps have been left behind according to charitable mandate, their collection is a matter of chance, of scavenging, of hand to mouth survival.

Derrida was usually generous to the intellectually hungry who followed him—he seems to have been able to regard even the mistaken uses that some made of his work as a kind of waste management. And followers like myself now have the privilege of gathering what got left along the way. These remainders may prove to be too scattered, too few, or too unseasonable to be widely useful. But Derrida had his own reservations about Heidegger's more deliberative "gathering" which "brings things together as one"—in this context "*Lesens*" should be translated as "harvesting" rather than "gleaning," for it is that which names, convokes, announces—which he came to identify as a gesture of logocentrism: "At bottom logocentrism is perhaps not so much the gesture that consists of putting logos at the center as the interpretation of logos as *Versammlung, that is a gathering* [*la rassemblement*] *that precisely concenters what it configures*" (*HE* 187, emphasis added).[16]

So, if Derrida meant to discard cultural graphology as fruit unfit for philosophical purpose, he might have smiled to see some of us eating it. Of course, you have to be careful, for if you snatch Derrida's thought up, without precaution, out of context, it is almost certain that very little of it will remain. And if you have exercised due caution, and have a good sense of what Derrida is likely to be doing, you will know, as a theoretical fact, that "what remains" is never a simple thing: "*restance* is never entirely restful," Derrida observed, "it is not substantial and insignificant presence" (*TP* 274). What remains for us is not a surviving part of what is gone, but a new relation to what was never entirely there.

Still, I am not first to have been attracted to this windfall. Close readers of *Grammatology* are few, and in English they are very few because Spivak's overly literal translation quickly baffles those who can't consult the original French. But those who persevere cannot fail to be struck by the fact that *Grammatology* appears to contain a tantalizing plan for future work. You can't mistake the fact that this could be no simple matter. Should we try to be grammatologists, or had we better content ourselves with doing cultural graphology? Is the aim to adopt a method, found a discipline, or begin to imagine the science of science? Did Derrida mean to encourage, or caution against, this work?

Among the three critics writing in English who have specifically advocated the development of Derrida's vision, there is little consensus on these and other matters, although—and this is fundamental, as I have already suggested—they each find themselves called to bring something other than deconstruction out of *Grammatology* by emphasizing the importance of writing within it. So, in *Applied Grammatology: Post(e) Pedagogy from Jacques Derrida to Jospeph Beuys*, Gregory Ulmer sought to replace deconstruction with grammatology by reading the work in relation to some of Derrida's other early writings, including *Writing and Difference* (1967), *Glas* (1974), and *The Truth in Painting* (1980).[17] In these works Ulmer found evidence to support his claim that the "goal" of grammatology should be "the reversal of phoneticization—the reduction of the phonetic in favor of the ideographic element in writing."[18] This attempt corresponds to the second of Derrida's topics for cultural graphology, where he called for new work within the "immense" and still scarcely broached field of the history of writing. As he elaborated this call in *Grammatology*, a new account of the history of writing would respect and afford space to the non-phonetic writing systems of other peoples, while working to understand the consequence of non-phonetic elements in our own (*Grammatology* 131–48). But Ulmer felt licensed to extrapolate Derrida's prompt into what he called a "practical extension of deconstruction"—that is, a form of creative thinking and experimental writing that used puns, homophones, and visual images to model nondiscursive thought, to "deconstruct the look of logocentrism," and to build "a coherent, productive procedure out of the elements of writing considered traditionally to be mere ornament."[19]

Ulmer worked very closely with Derrida's experimental writing in *Glas*, and like some other Anglo-American critics writing in the eighties and nineties, he allowed puns, metaphors, and other rhetorical figures to assume particular privilege in his own writing. Now, as the English might say, this sort of things is *all very well in France*, where the relations between rhetorical and logical argument are differently balanced, and where philosophy is written in a literary language that aims to please and provoke; it takes its puns and etymological associations seriously, if only to the extent that they are understood as a form of epistemological self-mockery.[20] But Anglo-American readers can't be expected to understand this, and by and large we don't. To the English-speaking detractors of Derrida's style (and of the "deconstructive method" it is thought to express) wordplay appears idle, or even superstitious, and when Ulmer suggests that Derrida's own *inventio* "functions on the assumption that language itself is intelligent, hence that homonyms 'know something,'" even well-disposed English readers such as myself will feel that he is claiming more for Derrida than Derrida claimed for himself.[21]

Derrida did argue that things could be written that could not be said. In response to the aphorism with which Wittgenstein closed his *Tractatus*, "Whereof one cannot speak, thereof one must be silent," Derrida replied with a formula that is now admired as an aphorism of his own: "What cannot be said above all must not be silenced but written" (*PC* 194).[22] He often sought to draw attention to the visual and aural dimensions of language as a way to encounter and counter the logocentric assumption that sophisticated instruments of signification must be "transparent," and in *Grammatology* he speculated that there might be something in literature that does not allow itself to be reduced to the voice, something that could be captured only by "isolating the bond that links the play of form to the substance of graphic expression" (*Grammatology* 59). This is what he had in mind, I think, when he advised those who would do cultural graphology to investigate the *becoming literary of the literal*: as he saw it, literature was a site where the graphic signifier *need not be "disdained*." Such were the grounds on which he admired Mallarmé, a writer who deployed the propensity of words to activate one another not only in rhyme schemes but also in visual patterns of placement and recurrence: "it is a production and a magnetization whose necessity imposes itself against contingency, arbitrariness, and semantic, or rather semiological haphazardness" (*D* 256).

In such uses, words admit new principles of organization and become, as Mallarmé claimed, "foreign to the language," even as they remain part of the "old language," and Derrida noted this effect as one for which he had use himself. In his own writing he explored the forms and etymologies of words as a way of thinking differently about concepts, and he used their material coincidences and accidents to stage the elements of undecidability and overdetermination within linguistic and other systems. In the decade after the publication of *Grammatology* Derrida even played with making his own name into a meaningful sign, "Derriere le Rideau"—[Derrida] behind the curtain.[23]

But let's note, as Ulmer did not, that Derrida is just as sensitive to aural as he is to visual patterns in language. Furthermore, nothing in his use of either of them suggests that he ever seriously approved the claim that such material coincidences speak to something deeper than themselves. The associative illogic of such games as he allowed himself was a philosophical provocation—a call to thought rather than a claim about how things are. If the expansion of his name could make it mean something veiled or hidden, this did not mean that Derrida had come to believe that his name *was* mysterious, only that a pun could turn a patronym into an occasion for marking the curious operation of names in general. Furthermore, the "new word," or the word newly foreign to the language as privileged and described by Mallarmé, "also *returns* to the language, recomposes with it according to new networks of differences, becomes divided up again, etc., in short, *does not become a master-word with the finally guaranteed integrity of a meaning or truth*" (*D* 256–57, emphasis added). Realizing that he had laid himself open to misunderstanding in relation to these issues, Derrida repeatedly warned against inverting the usual relationship between speech and writing in order to make letters the privileged repository of truth. Such a reversal, he insisted, would not correct or avoid logocentrism but only recoup, in the name of materiality, the idealism and humanism that it professed to escape.

Derrida's warning bears repeating here. Historians of the book may be surprised to discover that Derrida has some real claim to be counted among their number, and they will, I hope, be delighted and energized by the provocation of his dispersed observations about the materials of writing. But he should not be thought of as a "new materialist"; indeed, his writing can arm us to resist the romance with matter that is currently turning literary criticism towards a love of things. For, Derrida's concerns are semiotic; even when they are focused on the plastic properties of language (e.g., its extension, location, or duration), they are predicated on the assumption that information resides not in matter itself but in the differences that may be perceived between quantities and qualities within a given context. "Is it not evident that no signifier, whatever its substance and form, has a 'unique and singular reality'? A signifier is from the beginning the possibility of its own repetition, of its own image or resemblance. It is the condition of its ideality, what identifies it as the signifier, and makes it function as such, relating it to a signified which, for the same reason, could never be a 'unique and singular reality'" (*Grammatology* 91). If Derrida was interested in the instituted and fortuitous material resemblance between certain words, and the uses to which creative writers could put them, it was only as these might form the grounds for an accident that could produce "a kind of semantic mirage" and so "set something off"—a proposition very different from Ulmer's claim that homonyms "know things."[24]

In *Writing Matter: From the Hands of the English Renaissance* (1990) Jonathan Goldberg took a very different cue from Derrida's work. We might say that if Ulmer's aim was to *apply grammatology*, Goldberg's was to *do cultural graphology*. Citing the passages in *Grammatology* that most concern me in this introduction, he noted that they seem to sketch an itinerary that, "however much it represents the path not taken by Derrida," would nevertheless derive its program from Derrida's critique of writing.[25] As Goldberg sums it up, this critique calls for a rigorous analysis of where writing begins and ends; it draws attention to the ways in which western philosophy solves its own problems by an unthinking elevation of voice and by a corresponding repression of writing; and it challenges the ethnocentric assumption that some human groups are without writing because they do not use our own inscriptional techniques. But like others before and after him Goldberg worried that this critique is so general as to be overpowering: to say that all groups write is to run the risk of foreclosing historical and political considerations as to how, and with what consequences, writing systems are devised, regulated, and imposed on others. Rightly concluding that logocentrism can still be "delimited," and Derrida's critique of it pursued "in descriptions of writing that attend to the historical specificity of the regulation of writing in the narrow sense," Goldberg set out to trace the developing material and ideological practices of handwriting in early modern England in order to reveal "the social and historical embeddedness" of what is "variously defined as literacy, [and] of the institutions that promulgate and regulate its social instantiation and dispersion."[26]

Writing Matter thus pursues cultural graphology as a local science and in relation to the writing of early modern Europe—as such, it sounds much like my own project, for I have taken my examples from the work of sixteenth-century English printers. There is room in early-modern studies for two such projects, and for many more. The problem with practicing cultural graphology could never be that it had been done before, only that it could not be done enough. And its working method must have things in common with the logical procedure known as Ariadne's thread (oddly, perhaps, because the phrase actually describes what Theseus would have had to do if Ariadne's thread had snapped, leaving him to exhaustively explore every passage until he found the way back to the door on his own). For those whose labyrinth is an ethical or logical problem, the method is to keep trying while maintaining a record of exhausted options; and for those who would be cultural graphologists, the first gesture is perhaps to see what has been said about writing in various locales, even by other cultural graphologists, and then try something different. Carl Jung's famous warning to practitioners of psychotherapy bears repeating here: "each new case that requires thorough treatment is pioneer work, and every trace of routine then proves a blind alley . . . [it] is a most exacting business."[27]

And indeed my project has little in common with *Writing Matter*. Goldberg hoped his attention to the historic specificity of the regulation of Renaissance handwriting would contribute to a broader critique of logocentrism, and it is largely in this hope that *Writing Matter* identifies itself as cultural graphology; otherwise, it could be taken to be a sophisticated work of paleography and a straightforward contribution to the history of the book. My own project could not be so mistaken, for it is predicated on the proposition that ties cultural graphology to grammatology—that *we do not know what writing is*. A book historian who keeps this thought constantly in mind and uses it as the primary tool of her trade is not easily mistaken for one who does not.

The English-language project derived from *Grammatology* that has interested me the most is Christopher Johnson's *System and Writing in the Philosophy of Jacques Derrida*, a work that, like *Grammatology* itself, deserves to be more widely known.[28] Unlike Spivak, Johnson considers *écriture* (that is, "a general theory of writing as a fundamental structure of phenomena") to be "the most enduring element" of Derrida's philosophy. He argues that Derrida located his conception of writing within an intellectual paradigm that emerged after the Second World War to include the new sciences of information theory, communications technology, cybernetics, and molecular biology, a context within which the affinities of these sciences had become "so apparent" that Michel Serres was able to report that "we are once again beginning to dream of a *mathesis universalis* . . . . What biochemistry has discovered is not the mysterious noumenon, but quite simply a *universal science of the character*. Like the other sciences, it points towards a general philosophy of marked elements."[29] Johnson demonstrates Derrida's keen awareness that an understanding of combinatorial systems such as DNA formed a link between his own project and those of the new sciences. In *Grammatology* he remarked that "the contemporary biologist speaks of writing and *pro-gram* in relation to the most elementary processes of information within the living cell . . . [while] the entire field covered by the cybernetic *program* would be the field of writing" (*Grammatology* 9). Derrida understood that the benefit of this expanded sense of writing as it was becoming increasingly familiar in the late 1960s was that it opened a general field of inquiry within which both matter and différance (here understood as the proposition that there are no singular entities) could be understood as the constituents of, rather than as antonyms to, meaning.

Derrida's reconception of writing is useful to book historians because from small beginnings (that is, from writing "in the narrow sense") it broadens until it has transcended not only all forms of human agency but even the anthropological order itself, while beggaring the distinction, on which every other definition of writing continues to rely, between life and the technological extensions that make it possible. You might think that broadening writing to include everything will actually reduce it to nothing, and so prove not useful at all—others have said as much. But I have not found it to be so, and my own aim is to show how Derrida's expansive philosophical gestures can be cut into useful and purposeful sizes. Nothing in his thought requires us to take it, at each moment, to the limit. Indeed, one thing Derrida can teach us is that we will not, ever, reach the limit, and that work in both the arts and the sciences must proceed in the presence of questions that may never be answered. It is, however, precisely the shadow cast by these questions that makes the difference. And it is his commitment to thinking about their unaccountable impact on local circumstances that is the characteristic of Derrida's thought—his signature, we might say, had he not thought so hard about *that* as to render the idiom unwieldy.

Derrida called himself a historian and he had the local historian's love for the passing moment; his painstaking readings model what Nicholas Royle calls a "radical patience" that responds to the singularity of events within the contexts that give them meaning.[30] So in what follows I have not sought to push Derrida into places where a certain kind of thrill-seeking philosopher might hope to see metaphysics expiring (or perhaps failing to expire) in the darkness; nor have I any interest in using his work to bolster hopes that a rigorous study of letters may one day reveal itself to be a soft branch of the hard sciences. But I have found that his thoughtfulness is powerful in clearing some of the blocked passages that characterize areas of the literary criticism in which I was trained. Some of the conceptual tools that I have taken from Derrida and found most useful can also be picked up elsewhere—but for the sharpest of them all you still have to go to *Grammatology* and take into your own hands its simple but staggering proposal—*we do not know where writing begins and ends.*

It is because deconstruction interferes with solid structures, "material" institutions, and not only with discourses or signifying representations, that it is always distinct from an analysis or "critique."
«DERRIDA, *The Truth in Painting*, 19»

If the first challenge facing cultural graphology is to delimit its topics, the solution is to begin where you are. Since the field of my expertise is the writing culture of early modern England, particularly as it came to be influenced by the commercial development of print, it is there that I have looked for areas that would correspond to the four demarcated by Derrida: a psychopathology of writing that reconsidered and extended Freud's work in slips of the pen; a consideration of the non-phonetic elements of our own alphabetic system within what would then be a reconceived history of writing; a theory of the literary signifier that attended to the literality of the letter; and, finally, an initiative in what Derrida calls *psychoanalytic graphology*, a more general area that would use the insights of Melanie Klein to focus the concerns of the other three.[31]

I have tried to fulfill this schema in four chapters, each of which takes one of Derrida's leads and matches it with a bibliographical topic drawn from the area of early modern print work—specifically, (1) printed errors, (2) type ornament, (3) the practice of cutting print work with scissors and knives, and (4) black printed pages. Each chapter also takes one of Derrida's special terms and indicates its uses for historians of the book—specifically, (1) "différance," (2) "spacing," (3) "divisibility," and (4) "the archive." Finally, each chapter makes an argument that common sense and bibliographical expertise must judge to be simply wrong: (1) there is no such thing as an error in writing, (2) writing in its most general sense is something that cannot be seen, (3) there is no preservation, and (4) no one knows what paper is. My aim is not to prove these claims to be right (I have, after all, some common sense and some bibliographical expertise) but to demonstrate the thought that can be liberated at the position where they no longer seem wrong.

If I have scarcely departed from Derrida's blueprint in constructing this itinerary, I can't really claim to have followed it to the letter, for all that survives is the flimsiest of sketches, to consult which is like looking at a plan for a cathedral on an abandoned paper napkin. The directions contained in forty lines of *Writing and Difference* (230) are at once an expansion of the twenty-five that survive in *Grammatology* (87–88), and a contraction of its third chapter, "Of Grammatology as a Positive Science" (74–93), where Derrida explains why grammatology is at once necessary and precluded. But even in their most programmatic version in *Writing and Difference* they are obscure, telegraphic, and strangely truncated—Derrida says they are part of the synopsis of a lecture he gave four years earlier in a seminar conducted by André Green, when he was concerned to "open a debate" around issues he had raised in the review essay that became the first part of *Grammatology* (*WD* 246). To take guidance from a redaction of some of Derrida's earliest thought is like taking the First Quarto of *Hamlet* as the object of ten years of editorial labor, and I have had to ask myself if such a commitment is not a decision to *depart* from the thinker I ostensibly follow.

By way of restraining this impulse, I thought I might put Derrida's remarks in the local contexts I could reconstruct, in order to better understand what he may have meant.[32] I was interested to learn that his wife, Marguerite, was translating the work of Melanie Klein into French at the moment when he suggested that Klein's writing might "open the way" to the "new psychoanalytic graphology." It seemed important to me that Derrida's concern with the history of writing was occasioned, as Spivak notes, by the books whose review comprises much of the first half of *Grammatology*; and I hoped that the arrival of Julia Kristeva in Paris in 1966, the presence of Lacan, and Derrida's early contact with André Green and other analysts would explain his call for "a psychoanalysis of literature respectful of the originality of the literary signifier." But I came to realize that these contexts might inform, but could not govern, the direction of my work, and this for two reasons.

The first has to do with Derrida's prodigious energy and intellect, which meant that from the beginning of his career he brought to bear, on almost any topic, more learning than anyone could reasonably be expected to assemble in order to track his thought—more learning, even, than he had himself, for there are certainly moments in *Grammatology* and elsewhere where he seems to be channeling knowledge that he does not possess, like a young Bob Dylan singing dust bowl ballads. The second reason follows from the first, and is a defense against it: I am not a historian whose sole concern might be with where Derrida's ideas came from—rather, I am interested to discover where they might now go.[33] My aim has been to demonstrate the hitherto unrealized consequence of Derrida's blueprint for cultural graphology, and my hope is that others will join me in using it to release new values both within and beyond the study of literary texts.

1

The Psychopathology of Writing

Reviewing a book on children's toys, Walter Benjamin once observed that "a child wants to pull something, and so he becomes a horse; he wants to play with sand, and so he becomes a baker."[1] To achieve the expanded sense of writing that cultural graphology requires, we might start with a similar thought: A woman may pen a novel, fill out a form, or sign her name, not for an instrumental reason but because she wants to write. Then, effecting an even more radical displacement behind the appearance of things, we can go further and say that writing is the object of a set of actions whose aims are elsewhere, and now our woman writes to fill a gap or dominate an environment, or because she has an impulse to measure, stretch, cover, cut, fit, join, contain, open, close, begin, end, or repeat; to clear space or put something away so as not to have to think about it any longer; to reserve or store or spend; to pause, touch, or stroke . . . nothing can close this list. Perhaps she only wants to do or admire or join in; to follow or suffer or be herself. Perhaps she wants to love or—and this is a function of writing rarely adduced—perhaps her aim is *to leave things alone*. If each of these actions is an instance of *expression*, it is not the "self-expression" that is too easily attributed to writing but the articulation of life lived at the place where we happen to be.

To have come so far is by no means to have reached the end of what Derrida means by writing—you are only in its outskirts. But already it seems unlikely that all this could be fenced within the realm of psychology. Indeed, such constraint would be *ungrammatological*. Countering Saussure's argument that "it is for the psychologist to determine the exact place of semiology" Derrida urged that research on the sign *not* be confined to the psyche (*Po* 21). And those who read *Grammatology* with care can see that the study of writing envisaged there would finally extend to cover *all information in the biosphere* (where information is any reliable material covariance, and the biosphere understood not as an entity but as a process of the reception and exchange of this information).

But cultural graphology needs limits, and it is in Derrida's own blueprint that, if psychoanalysis must always fall short of being grammatology, it should nevertheless be granted a controlling interest over the local topics and issues that would make up the more worldly and feasible science that concerns us here. And it seems prudent enough to begin, as he suggested, with a *psychopathology of writing in general* that would not limit itself to slips of the pen but would still pay more rigorous attention to them than Freud did himself. This is a prudent enough strategy—as long as we are aware from the start that, in Derrida's reading, psychoanalysis will turn out to know *a great deal more than it knows it knows about writing* and a great deal about what Derrida once called the "techno-political history" of the book (*PM* 13).

If Derrida's relations with the thinkers he admired were often vexed, his early ambivalence towards Freud, and his need to put an effective distance between psychoanalysis and deconstruction, was especially marked. In 1988 he shocked an audience at the Sorbonne by declaring to René Major "I have never subscribed to any proposition of psychoanalysis." Geoffrey Bennington, who tells this story, notes that you could be forgiven for thinking otherwise. "Does he not say," ponders Bennington, "for example in *Of Grammatology*, that the best chances of achieving a breakthrough with respect to metaphysics are to be found, alongside linguistics, in psychoanalysis?" Was it not Freud who first gave voice to Derrida's proposition "that the present in general, is not primal but, rather, reconstituted . . . that there is no purity of the living present?" (*WD* 212). And doesn't Derrida "appeal all over the place" to Freudian conceptuality? Furthermore, if it is true, as Derrida says, that none of Freud's concepts escape metaphysics, it is also true that for him *no* concept does. What could be the reason, then, for this outspoken *resistance* to psychoanalysis? Bennington answers, for Derrida, that while psychoanalysis may come very close to deconstruction, and look like it too, what it has not yet done, and may never be able to do, is "elucidate the law of its own belonging to metaphysics." And he imagines Derrida ruling on the matter: "not really thinking through both the necessary belonging of its concepts to the history of metaphysics and its necessary strategic displacement of those concepts, psychoanalysis *understands less* than deconstruction."[2]

If the judgment ventriloquized here does not do justice to psychoanalysis (Bennington himself describes Freud trying to reshape and displace the metaphysical concepts, inadequate to his purpose, with which he was working in *Beyond the Pleasure Principle*), it is also not completely fair to Derrida, whose mid-career reading of that late text matches Bennington's as he describes how Freud's thought "advanced, only to suspend without any possibility of stopping, all those theses in which his successors or heirs and readers in general would have had him stop" (*R* 41).

As he grew older Derrida felt an increasing admiration for and kinship with Freud, and, at this late moment, as he describes the founder of psychoanalysis eluding the constructions that his followers want to put on his thought, he could be talking of himself. But as a younger scholar Derrida found that the question of *the stopping point*, of the limit that allows every inquiry to proceed, was not so easily suspended. In *Grammatology* you can find him facing the formidable problem of delimitation in relation to his own method of reading Rousseau. And here his response is to deflect attention from his own difficulties to those, presumably worse, that a psychoanalytic reading would have in deciding between what truly belonged to Rousseau as his own "proper" thoughts and what we might once have called their "context":

> Around the irreducible point of the originality of this writing an immense series of structures, of historical totalities of all orders, are organized, enveloped, and blended. Supposing psychoanalysis could, in principle, succeed in outlining and interpreting them, supposing that it could take into account the entire history of Western metaphysics as it offers habitation to, and enters into relations with, Rousseau's text, it would still have to describe the law of its *own* belonging to metaphysics and to western culture. Let us not pursue this any further. We have already measured the difficulty of the task and the element of frustration in our own interpretation of the supplement. We are sure that *something* irreducibly Rousseauist is captured there but we have carried off at the same time an unformed mass of roots, soil, and sediments of all sorts. (*Grammatology* 161, translation modified)

If psychoanalysis could describe absolutely everything that surrounds and determines an act of writing, and if it could, in addition, describe its own place within metaphysics, then it would no longer be psychoanalysis but an ideal form of deconstruction. But faced with the task of sketching out what psychoanalysis cannot and will not be able to explain, Derrida's energy fails him: "Let us not," he says, "pursue this any further." We can't blame him—but neither can we help noticing that the problem here has less to do with psychoanalysis than the fact that he has *already* "measured the difficulty" and described the "frustration" of trying to account for a thing in relation to its total context *in his own interpretation of the supplement*: "we are sure that *something* irreducibly Rousseauist is captured there but we have carried off at the same time an unformed mass of roots, soil, and sediments of all sorts."

The question of where to stop is rarely faced so squarely. Derrida never found an answer for it, but he continued to think about it. Where to stop contextualizing (this is the problem encapsulated by his infamous claim that "there is nothing outside the text"); where to stop analyzing (because the point comes where we have to get on with thinking, albeit with conceptual tools inadequate to the task); where to stop assigning responsibility (because, as every parent knows, we can attend responsibly to one thing only at the expense of others)? There is no proper accounting for anything if you cut it short, and there is no accounting for anything if you do not cut it short. And here you can see Derrida broaching the ethical issues that became the more articulate concern of his later years—for, to focus on context is to focus on responsibility, and to focus on responsibility is to focus on context.

Deconstruction and psychoanalysis thus have in common that *both want to* and *neither can* delimit their topics or think through the necessary belonging of their concepts to the history of metaphysics—with the result that they both quickly get to the point where their task is to indicate what we may never know: "There is at least one spot in every dream at which it is unplumbable," said Freud, "a navel, as it were, that is its point of contact with the unknown" (*SE* 4:111). And Freud produced another image to explain why the interpretation of a dream is always curtailed: "The dream thoughts . . . cannot, from the nature of things, have any definite endings; they are bound to branch out in every direction into the intricate network of our world of thought. It is at some point where this network is particularly dense that the dream wish grows up, like a mushroom out of its mycelium" (*SE* 5:525). That a thought or an entity is a mushroom growing from a mycelium of other thoughts or entities—this is what Derrida means by *dissemination*.

That *every* train of interpretative thought has therefore to be broken off, that even deconstruction must "outline" and thereby deracinate the things it would interpret is common sense. But in 1967 Derrida still felt there were places where Freud could be blamed for having cut his inquiries too short and for giving up the chase just when things were getting interesting. He says so twice in "Freud and the Scene of Writing," once when he suggests we should be "more attentive" to the slip of the pen "and to its originality" than Freud ever was, and again when he lands heavily on Freud's remark that while the mystic writing pad models the structure of the psychic apparatus, it cannot imitate its live functioning. "It would be a mystic pad indeed if, like our memory, it could accomplish that," smiled Freud (*SE* 19:230). "All that Freud had thought about the unity of life and death should have led him to ask other questions here," says Derrida, not smiling (*WD* 227–30).

What did he mean? If we rephrase "the unity of life and death" as *the essential relation of the living to the non-living*, we seem to be face-to-face with the familiar "question of technology." And it *would* be familiar were Derrida not calling for its reconception: "here the question of technology (a new name must perhaps be found in order to remove it from its traditional problematic) may not be derived from an assumed opposition between the psychical and the nonpsychical, life and death." Writing in its most general form, "arche-writing," is the name that Derrida gives to technology conceived in this way, as a system or program that subtends and only secondarily produces distinctions between the living and the nonliving, between the present and representation, or—as we could say, though Derrida does not—between meaning (which is constructed by something living) and information (which requires nothing more than reliable material covariance). The "question of technology" is thus "the question of writing"—and one that neither Derrida nor the rest of us will ever be done with. It follows that "that which, in Freud's discourse, opens itself to the theme of writing results in psychoanalysis not being simply psychology—nor simply psychoanalysis" (*WD* 228). And if psychoanalysis should have a "controlling interest" in the new discipline of cultural graphology, that is because psychoanalysis itself is finally "controlled" (at least, it is everywhere destabilized) by its own entanglements with the themes and techniques of writing in both its narrow and broader senses.

A psychopathology of writing such as Derrida called for in his blueprint for cultural graphology would thus comprise everything within the discourse of psychoanalysis that Freud had thought, as well as everything that he had failed to think, about writing and the ways in which psychical impulses are recorded and archived. It would lead over familiar ground onto some much less travelled and more challenging terrain, to the point where the energies and competencies of our individual disciplines would begin to fail.

Derrida cut a path in this direction in 1995 with *Archive Fever: A Freudian Impression*; two years later he was still mulling over the issues he encountered there in an interview he gave to the journal *Les Cahiers de médiologie* for a special issue on the powers of paper. In these two works his thoughts about writing are under immense and special pressure, for there is nothing without writing; no writing without the preservation offered, however briefly, by an archive; and no archive that is not the immediate destruction (either by oblivion, or by an opening to the future) of what is preserved. To have archive fever is thus to have no rest "from searching for the archive right where it slips away" (*AF* 91). Derrida testified that he had contracted this fever as an adolescent, and he was never able to shake its anguishing consequences: "If I love the word," he told a conference of translators in 1998, "it is only in the body of its idiomatic singularity, where a passion for translation comes to lick it as might a flame or an amorous tongue" (WRT 175).[3]

I will return to these hectic texts in my final chapter, for in 1967 there was one topic that Derrida could immediately name as needing more attention, and that was the *lapsus calami*. Freud's claim was that writing errors result when unconscious impulses attach themselves to, and interfere with, conscious intentions. Compromise formations that can be read as the expression of unconscious wishes, they are a subset of the bungled actions, or parapraxes, that we now recognize as "Freudian slips." But you can see why Derrida found the remarks that concluded Freud's extensive analysis of slips of the voice to be provoking: "*Slips of the pen*, to which I now pass, are so closely akin to slips of the tongue that we have nothing new to expect from them" (*SE* 15:69).[4] Derrida's first thought would have been that writing errors can't be subsumed to those of the voice, for the pen can write things the tongue cannot say; his second that Freud himself likened the psyche to a script that has never been "subject to, never exterior and posterior to, the spoken word" (*WD* 209).

But is there more to the topic than an opportunity to correct this expression of Freud's phonocentrism? In the brief remarks we are considering Derrida observed only one more thing—namely, Freud's self-restriction in the matter of pen slips "did not prevent him from raising the fundamental juridical problem of responsibility, before the tribunal of psychoanalysis, for example in relation to the murderous *lapsus calami*."[5] "Questions of Responsibility" was the overarching title under which Derrida conducted his teaching seminars after 1991. The topics he addressed under this rubric (which include testimony, hospitality, eating, animals, sovereignty, and the death penalty) allowed him to give pointed expression to the question of what it means to respond to, before, or on behalf of another; they also consolidated the position of those who want to see an "ethical turn" in his career. But an interest in responsibility is evident in Derrida's earliest writing: it can be found, as I have already indicated, in the question of context, and also in the form of the pressing disciplinary question of what becomes of philosophical responsibility once the most basic certainties of its discourse have been shown to have motives and attachments of which it remains unaware. Still, it might be *just as true*—and just as true to Derrida—to say that he *never* had any interest in responsibility, and that this lack of interest, which takes the form of a deep suspicion of anyone who claims to have arrived at a position of ethical or disciplinary responsibility without noticing that every such position involves *irresponsibility towards other others*, is already fully evident in *Writing and Difference*.

And within that volume, in "Freud and the Scene of Writing," the very essay that contains Derrida's blueprint for cultural graphology, the idea that we might be held individually responsible for what we write is foreclosed even before there is any question of an unconsciously motivated slip of the pen. For Derrida argues that the subject who writes is neither sovereign nor single but "a *system* of relations" between the "strata" that constitute the psyche, society, and the material world. Or, as he puts it later, "one must be several in order to write" (*TP* 152). If historians of the book and sociologists of the text must continue to use the blunt concepts of author and reader, an account of "the *sociality* of writing" as the drama of the interplay of these strata in their historical relations would, he remarks, require "an entirely different discipline" (*WD* 227). Another name for this discipline, which would combine (at the very least) psychoanalysis, literary history, bibliography, book history, the sociology of texts, and information technology, is, of course, cultural graphology.

It is probably safe to say, then, that what drew Derrida to Freud's work on the bungled actions of which we are all guilty was not so much its account of the lapsus calami as its extraordinary attempt to describe individual human actions within the tangled web of the material and immaterial systems that are their total context. A pen slip is certainly a useful example of such an action because it is immediately archived in a preservable form from which it can be retrieved and used in evidence against us. The more interesting point, however, is that *the archive is part of the action* in that it is, at least in part, the cause of what it registers. Of course Freud knew that the material properties of words (the fact that, in whole or in part, one looks or sounds like many others) are part of the circumstances within which linguistic errors occur. What he did not allow, but what his examples everywhere show, is that language is a system of small differences whose processing means that it is never not reactive to these circumstances. (If you can feel a headache coming on here this is the beginning of archive fever, the burning fact that every act of registration, without which nothing happens, changes and so destroys what it takes into its care.)

In 1974 Sebastiano Timpanaro took serious and careful issue with Freud's proposition that the unconscious was the agent of linguistic errors. The thrust of his argument concerned the status of the so-called associative links that, according to Freud, attached conscious and unconscious intentions within a given scribal error. As Freud saw it, the two intentions might be related through a shared content—in which case the disturbing intention would contradict, correct, or supplement that which it disturbed, as when an estranged husband wrote to invite his American wife to join him in Europe and recommended that she travel not (as he had meant to write) on the Mauretania but on the Lusitania, a passenger ship that had been torpedoed in 1915 (*SE* 15: 34). In most cases, however, the associative link lay not in the content of the two intentions but was, as Freud puts it, "artificially constructed" along paths forged using the graphic and phonetic similarities or strained conceptual kinships between words, as when a woman anxious for children always read "storks" for "stocks," or when Freud himself, the inveterate collector, read "antiquities" on every shop sign that showed the "slightest resemblance" to the word (*SE* 15:62–63).

Timpanaro did not deny that some verbal slips were caused by the interference of unconscious wishes, but he pointed out that many of the errors Freud analyzed were *typical* instances of the scribal or typographical gaffes with which proofreaders such as himself were only too familiar: repetitions, omissions, perseverations, anticipations, the transpositions of phonically or semantically similar words, the replacement of terms by their opposites, the (very common) omission or introduction of negatives, and *banalization* (the replacement of hard terms with those more familiar). He concluded that what Freud regarded as *Begünstigungen* (the material circumstances that favored but did not cause the slip of tongue, pen, or memory) were often sufficient conditions for the error in question. In which case he felt it should be identified not as a parapraxis (which is the expression of an unconscious wish) but rather as a counterproduction, a chance effect that results when a physiological weakness such as tiredness causes a speaker or scribe to confuse the material or ideational properties of words.[6]

Freud had anticipated this objection to his theory, and in the second of his *Introductory Lectures* he invoked the problem of recurrent or obstinate misprints (which could, he felt, be regarded as "'writing mistakes' on the compositor's part") to draw attention to a class of parapraxes that cannot be explained as resulting from physiological inattention or failure. For here the error appears, or reappears, in the very place where we are doing our best to avoid it. "In such cases," says Freud, "people speak of a 'demon of misprints' or a 'type-setting fiend'—terms which at least go beyond any psycho-physiological theory of misprints" (*SE* 15:31). Freud often made recourse to folk wisdom, or found in literature and myth an acknowledgement of the unconscious thoughts that we otherwise prefer to disavow, but the printers' devil is a curious story to have chosen here, for this special demon is said to have haunted workshops using moveable type, and its invocation suggests that the cause of writing errors should be sought not in the overmastering of an individual psyche by an unconscious thought but rather in the social and technological drama of the print room.

Freud had already noted how difficult it is to find the single person responsible for a printed error. How tempting for a workman to believe himself innocent, how easy to deflect the blame! The finger of suspicion could point to the compositor, as Freud thought, but behind his efforts lie those of the operative, usually an apprentice, whose job is to redistribute the type back into the compartments from which each character was drawn: if he has carelessly put a letter in the wrong compartment, the compositor will use it without knowing the difference. As for the proofreader, his duties will be divided between loyalty to the copy from which the type was set and a desire to make clean and clear sense of what was on it; and the difficulty of his task may be brought home to us if we consider that he will be confronted by hidden errors—those that are invisible to the proofreader as they make their own local sense.[7]

Nevertheless, Freud recounts the case, suggested to him by Steckel, of what he considers to be a revealing blunder in a widely circulated weekly paper. It concerns a vindication of the paper written with great warmth by a staff writer, approved by the Editor-in-Chief, and read in proof more than once. "Everybody was satisfied, when the printer's reader suddenly noticed a slight error that had escaped the attention of all. There it was, plainly enough: 'Our readers will bear witness to the fact that we have always acted in a selfish manner for the good of the community'"

(*SE* 6:126). Freud does not recount who took the fall for this. But does it much matter which member of staff first omitted the negative? In such situations everyone involved feels personally responsible *and* personally exonerated (if the error happened on my watch, I did not make it; someone else should have noticed I had not noticed it; besides, there is something in the truth we have inadvertently pinned to ourselves, for whether we are acting for ourselves or for the good of the community we are always acting *at the expense of other others*, and this truth is the foundation of a sophisticated and reputable ethics . . .).

Since the question of responsibility is always everywhere, Derrida's suggestion that, in relation to writing errors, it might be addressed in the first instance to the "murderous *lapsus calami*" is artificially heightened. Besides, as Freud read them, bungled actions of all kinds reveal the unconscious competitive or libidinous aims of their perpetrators, and it would be hard to say that any of the parapraxes he describes are *not* finally oedipal, and therefore "murderous"—a claim that holds true even of the unconsciously motivated instances of self-injury that form a somber lining to the human comedy of the *Psychopathology*.[8] It is true that in the later *Introductory Lectures* Freud does suggest other motives for parapraxes—for example, that a "psychical flight from unpleasure" might be the "ultimate operative motive" for many a blunder, as when we unconsciously avoid a word or letter that may trigger an uncomfortable memory; he also noted that common pen slips, such as contractions and anticipations, point to "a general dislike of writing and a desire to be done with it." And we might think of this desire *to be done with writing* (which, when you think about it, structures, if it does not govern, every act of writing), as the expression of a death-driven impulse *to be done with everything*—an impulse that could then be split into the apocalyptic wish *that everything be done with*, and a less drastic and more realistic hope *that someone else does it* [SE 15:75, 69]). But the flight from disturbance, which characterizes the pleasure principle in Freud's early work, is rarely noted in the *Psychopathology*, where Freud tends to read parapraxes as being wedded, almost exclusively, to the expression of immoral libidinal wishes, including the desire to kill.

All the same, however general the "murderous" intent of parapraxes, Freud is strikingly reluctant to discuss cases where unconscious intentions cause real harm to others, and he adduces only two instances of writing errors that manifest what he calls "practical importance"—namely, the case of a doctor who prescribed belladonna to three elderly women in preparations of dangerous strength and the pen slip of the murderer H., who accidentally revealed his plans when ordering bacterial pathogens from a laboratory for "experiments on men" (*Menschen*), rather than, as he had intended to write, for experiments on mice and guinea pigs (*Mausen oder Meerschweinchen*) (*SE* 6:122–25; *SE* 15:69–70). Each of these mistakes expressed injurious intentions, Freud thought, but the doctor caught each one before it was too late, and none of these cases revealed "whether these thoughts were to be taken as a clear intention to injure, or as a phantasy of no practical importance" (*SE* 15:70).

In fact, although Freud takes no account of it, H. had *already acted* on his murderous impulses—if he hadn't yet killed anyone, that was why he was writing to the directors of the laboratory: to complain that the preparation sent him had proved too weak for the purpose. It was thus the desire to confess, rather than to murder, which remained unconscious with him.[9] But this is not Freud's concern, for here he directs the question of responsibility not to the murderer but to the recipients of his letter—should they not have seen that his slip was a confession and prevented further killings? The problem is that an unconscious thought may have no practical consequence, either for the subject, or for those within his reach; had he been accused of murderous wishes before he first acted on them H. might have been able to claim, with perfect truth, that nothing was further from his conscious intention (*SE* 15:70).

The popularity of the *Psychopathology* can be attributed to the skill with which Freud draws us into feeling a communal responsibility for blunders that any one of us could make, while sparing us their consequences. Within his illustrative anecdotes, disreputable wishes are usually diagnosed and punctured, and thoughts of death noted and deflected, before anyone has been seriously harmed, while more upsetting events, such as that of a circus performer who drowned her husband by misplacing the key to the chains that bound him underwater, are taken from literary sources, so that, as we can tell ourselves, they have not actually happened (*SE* 6:188–89). But if keeping a clear distinction between destructive fantasies and their real-life consequence was part of Freud's expository purpose, his final point, and the thrust of his work elsewhere, is that there is no way of living that keeps the two apart. Accidents appear to be objective happenings but "you would hardly believe how difficult it sometimes is" to tell them apart from subjective acts, since "an act so often understands how to disguise itself as a passive experience" (*SE* 15:58). It has, we feel, perhaps been committed "accidentally on purpose," which is why we typically think that our friends cannot be blamed and yet should accept some responsibility for the painful accidents that befall them.

Ernest Jones spelled out this curious judgment of responsibility in his elaboration of Freud's work on printed errors:

> In the notorious Wicked Bible, issued in 1631, the word "not" was omitted from the Seventh Commandment, so that this read: "Thou shalt commit adultery." The possibility is not to be excluded that the editor had a personal interest in the subject of the commandment. At all events he was heavily fined, it being empirically recognized that whether his purpose was conscious or unconscious he was equally responsible for it, and that he had no right, even "accidentally," to impute such commandments to Jahve.[10]

This is a motivated reading—one that the mischievous could ascribe to Jones's own adulterous impulses—for both he and Freud knew perfectly well that disturbances in writing do not often spell out the content of the unconscious wishes that caused them: Freud carefully explained that in most cases their sense can be discovered, if at all, only by following a chain of semantic or material displacements back to the disturbing thought.[11]

But since this is the case, what are we to make of the fact that Freud included this anecdote within his own work, and was equally facetious in accounting for another printed error?

> Another biblical misprint dates back to the year 1580, and is found in the Bible of the famous library of Wolfenbuttel, in Hesse. In the passage in Genesis where God tells Eve that Adam shall be her master and shall rule over her, the German translation is "Und er soll dein Herr sein." The word Herr (master) was substituted by Narr, which means fool. Newly discovered evidence seems to show that the error was a conscious machination of the printer's suffragette wife, who refused to be ruled by her husband. (*SE* 6:127)

These are not just any jokes. In the first Jones pretends to believe in the licentious unconscious impulses of the master printer; in the second Freud posits a wife who consciously alters her husband's print work. If each appears to be poking fun at the unsatisfactory institution that is marriage, the real frivolity is that in neither case is the analyst taking his own argument seriously. It is as if each one *saw without seeing* (as Derrida would say) that printers' errors will not easily yield up the unconscious impulses that caused them and decided to crack a joke rather than face the consequence of what they had seen.

What these jokes seek to deny is the recalcitrance of the field of writing to psychoanalytic rule. The problem that pen slips pose to the analyst—one that is underlined when the error occurs in the complex genesis of print work—is that he *can't* know when he is faced with a circumstantial rather than with a psychically motivated mistake (this, I think, is why Freud sometimes admitted, and sometimes denied, that some slips of the pen were just that). More troubling still is the fact that you can never be certain that a motivated error has *not* occurred, for *any* minor inconsistency in print work may be a parapraxis, although its meaning and even its presence may never be known to anyone. Indeed, although Freud does not admit it, even a successful performance of accuracy could be a symptom of psychopathology—who could say otherwise? André Green's modification of Freud's work will help us here, as it may have helped Derrida with "Freud and the Scene of Writing," which was first presented as a lecture in Green's seminar. Green's position, as he put it later, was that "we have underestimated the healthy aspect" and "over-emphasized the pathological aspect" of the fact that, in all of us, and in spite of the censorship of our reason, "repressed wishes succeed in finding satisfaction through a special mode of thought designed to ensure the victory of the pleasure principle." [12] The primary and secondary processes are complementary in addition to being in competition with each other, and the effective functioning of a normal person is, in each case, the happily compromised formation of a private madness.

And here we have the payoff from Derrida's suggestion that we pursue a psychopathology of writing through and beyond Freud's brief consideration of pen slips. For we can now see that *every* act of writing is more or less pathological, in the broadened sense that we will now have to give this term, and that each text, even before we undertake our own pathological processes of *misreading* it, is *parapraxis all the way down.*[13] If this appears to strengthen Freud's argument to the point where it disappears, it also allows us to better understand his argument in the *Psychopathology* that *there are no errors.*

It does not take much to recognize this statement as another version of what Derrida means by dissemination. Noting, in *The Truth in Painting*, that Freud sometimes understands the shoe as a substitute for the phallus, and sometimes as a symbol of the female genitals, Derrida reminds us that the meanings of dream-symbols vary "according to the circumstances, in other words also according to a syntax irreducible to any semantic or 'symbolic' substantiality." It is, he concludes, "always necessary to hold in reserve a sort of excess of interpretation, a supplement of reading—which is decisive, to tell the truth—for the idiom of a syntactic variation." In writing, as in dream work, it does not matter what a thing is, nor even what it can symbolize; the determining factor is how, and in what circumstances, it is used, where every use is not only a "variant" of, but also a variant from, the "universal" symbol. In short, we are *always* concerned with "variations which are also deviations [*écarts*], restructurations, general redistributions. And deviations *without* an essential *norm*. Network of differential traces" (*TP* 268–69).

In the final chapter of the *Psychopathology* Freud describes himself writing a letter to Fliess in which he said that, having corrected the proofs, he was now sending *The Interpretation of Dreams* to press and would not make any more changes, "even if it contains 2,467 mistakes" (*SE* 6:242). His joke here concerns his own argument that it is impossible to think of a random number (think of a number, any number, and you will find your choice had unconscious motivations), but the anecdote shows that he too knew all along that typographical errors were so legion as to be matters of indifference to the wise.[14]

Early modern readers, who encountered printed works that were (as it has been the pleasure of recent book historians to demonstrate) anything but fixed, expected their own books to contain variants and errata. Most were content to overlook them, while others may have enjoyed the task of correcting them. In 1658, in a typical comment that notes "no books are printed without some faults," John Heydon cautioned each man to "look into himself before he despises another," and sensibly suggested that readers "either allow or amend" such errors as they were bound to find.[15] The errata lists that frequently appear at the end of printed books may appear to modern eyes to be the expression of guilt or frustration on the part of the printer, but they are also an indication of the expectation of proofreaders who had begun a process of correction designed to attract the energies of the reader into improving the text for themselves and others.

So what was it that drew a heavy fine onto the head of the King's Printer Robert Barker for his omission of a negative in the seventh commandment? The story as Jones tells it is a good one, but the punishment was actually imposed not because the missing negative was recognized as a manifestation of Barker's unconscious adulterous desires but for the "many grosse errors and foule faults committed in the printing of the holy bible." The punishment, which was subsequently converted into a requirement that Barker procure Greek types and matrices and engage in the painstaking and unprofitable work of printing a Greek volume every year at his own expense for as long as he held the lucrative Bible patent, expresses a general sense that those entrusted with the patent were taking less care, employing less skilled craftsmen, and using worse quality paper and ink than the task demanded or than its profitable nature made reasonable.[16] And if the commandment to commit adultery was the final straw in this context, it was not because it was considered to be a revealing personal gaffe but because it represented a desecration of Scripture that scandalously diverted it from its sacred meaning, causing an offence all the more violent for being excessive in relation to anything that had "objectively" happened, and particularly hard to overlook in the Decalogue, whose Ten Commandments were said to have been "written with the finger of God" on the two tables of stone entrusted to Moses on Mount Sinai (Exod. 31).[17]

But there is something else to consider. Appearing at the very point where it is most important to get things right, the statement "Thou shalt commit adultery" demonstrates that even Scripture is vulnerable to human error and machine failure during the processes of its reproduction. It also draws attention to the unsettling fact that if it is to occur in language (which is to say if it is to be transmitted at all), the Word of God must be structured like other words, and therefore own a propensity to deviate—not just because language can't say what it means, or because its material forms leave it open to frequent accidents, but because words and letters are signs *only* to the extent that each is not linked to a single meaning and can be repeated elsewhere and otherwise, legible each time through the differential relation it establishes with the new linguistic elements among which it is placed. The four words "thou," "shalt," "commit," and "adultery" have been accurately transmitted, but into a context where if they continue to perform their old function they radically, scandalously, upend it.

In "Mes Chances," an essay that picks up where "Freud and the Scene of Writing" leaves off, Derrida muses over the fact that "language is only one among those systems of marks that *simultaneously* incline towards increasing the reserves of random indetermination *as well as* the capacity for coding and over-coding or, in other words, for control and self-regulation" (MC 2–3). Christopher Johnson offers a useful elaboration of this point: "this strange tendency of all dynamic systems to combine chance and necessity, coding and indetermination, means that they are necessarily conservative (the condition of their existence and persistence) but equally inherently unstable (the condition of their dynamism)."[18] A dynamic system is one that works and survives through its capacity to change in relation to its environment—its code or program is never simply present but is a tendency or opportunity that manifests itself through the very circumstances it transforms. The combination of DNA, which contributes to the hereditary processes of evolution *because* it contains within itself the possibility for chance mutation, with RNA, which carries out or expresses this genetic coding, is perhaps the clearest example of such system, and language is another almost as clear. But if we can use Derrida's own expanded sense of the term, the general name for the totality of these dynamic, nonlinear systems would be *writing*.

Beneath thought, beneath error, beneath all forms of transmission and inheritance lies site-specific variance. Freud's interest in the occurrence of errors in the places where they are least welcome led him to observe this phenomenon twice in relation to the question of print, although each is a peculiar form of variance that Freud stages as a by-product of a compulsion to repeat. We have already encountered one of these instances, the typesetting fiend. But in 1919 Freud added a story to the *Psychopathology* to exemplify further the operation of "obstinate" errors. Taken from a biography of the dramatist Frank Wedekind, it describes one actor's attempt to do justice to a solemn line in his autobiographical play *Die Zensur* (The Censorship), "The fear of death is an intellectual error [*Denkfehler*]." The first night the actor declaimed "The fear of death is a *Druckfehler* [a printed error]." Advised of his blunder, on the second night he managed "The fear of death is a *Denkzettel* [a memorandum]." Corrected once again, on the third night he announced "the fear of death is a *Druckzettel* [a printed label]."

A parapraxis that repeats in this way, changing its form while the outcome remains the same, gives a "vivid impression," says Freud, of a will "unknown to consciousness" that is "striving for a definite aim" (*SE* 6:236–38). We are faced here with an opportunity such as Derrida relished, positioned to think more deeply about writing than Freud did. In this case we can glean from Freud a reflection on writing that supports Derrida's own sense of its ubiquitous consequence as a dynamic and differential system that beggars not only the distinction between the life and the death instincts (for this is Freud's own position in *Beyond the Pleasure Principle*) but between that which is alive and that which is not.

So what can we make of the curious fatality whereby terms concerning the materials of thought (*Denk*) and error (*Fehler*) are first incrementally, and then finally, displaced by those of writing (print [*Druck*] and paper [*Zettel*])? Of course the anecdote is an *illustration* of what Freud identifies as an unconscious prompting, not the thing itself. But if the story is to be believed, Wedekind, who rapidly forgave and befriended the young actor, understood what Freud did not—namely, that the drive towards linguistic variance is a force stronger, more general, and more basic, more demonic even, than the unconscious impulses that make use of it.

2

Type Ornament

It is less a question of confiding new writings to the envelope of a book than of finally reading what wrote itself between the lines in the volumes. That is why, beginning to write without the line, one begins also to reread past writing according to a different organization of space.
«Derrida, *Grammatology*, 86–87»

The consequence of Derrida's advice that we attend to the non-phonetic elements within our own phonetic system cannot be overestimated.[1] Phonocentrism is the belief that, since alphabetic writing represents the spoken voice, it is both the norm and the cream of writing systems, and for Derrida this conviction is the single problem underlying all the fields that would comprise grammatology. A problem in two senses. On the one hand it is the topic with which grammatology should be most concerned: "the continuous vein that circulates through all these fields of reflection and constitutes their fundamental unity is the problem of the phoneticization of writing" (*Grammatology* 88). On the other hand phoneticization is, simply, a big problem. Hand in glove with the metaphysics of presence, organizing human experience according to what is claimed to be the irreversibility of sound and suppressing everything that might resist the assumptions of its own linear logics, phoneticization is the loudmouthed ethnographer who can't recognize other people's writing systems, the philosopher who crushes the thought of his students with his own certainties, the scientist who refuses to recognize the metaphors by which her thought is constrained. It is for this reason that Derrida points out that, in actual fact, "phonetic" and "nonphonetic" have never been "pure qualities of certain systems of writing," rather "they are the abstract characteristics of typical elements, more or less numerous and dominant within all systems of signification in general" (*Grammatology* 89).

Christopher Norris sensibly suggested that a consideration of "punctuation, spacing, diacritical marks and so forth" would meet Derrida's brief to attend to the non-phonetic elements in our own system.[2] But since that brief is (at least in the first place) a call to identify and begin to give and take some account of forms of information transfer that do not pass through the voice, it is a problem that most diacritical marks are glyphs added to letters to *change their pronunciation*, which is to say that their primary function is to register the sounds of language. Punctuation's case is not much better. The question of whether its purpose is grammatical or elocutionary—whether it aims to show what a sentence means or, alternatively, how it should be spoken—was not settled in England before the end of the eighteenth century: in 1795 Lindley Murray's best-selling *English Grammar, Adapted to the Different Class of Learners* still described punctuation as "the art of dividing a written composition into sentences, or parts of sentences, by points or stops, for the purpose of marking the different pauses which the sense, and an accurate pronunciation, require."[3] Even Ben Jonson, credited with having been the first to call for a logical English punctuation, aimed only to *add* this function to its already elocutionary purpose. His *English Grammar* surveys and recommends the use of logical punctuation, but it continues to remind readers that prosody and control of the breath are not just parts of grammar "but diffus'd, like the blood, and spirits, through the whole."[4]

As Jonson's image suggests, few elements of alphabetic writing can be isolated from the influence of speech. Handwriting styles or font size and design, numerals, the difference between upper and lower case letters, underlining, italics, and some other elements of layout are more obvious manifestations of non-phonetic impulses than are either punctuation or diacritical marks, but even many of these conventions could be argued to have derived from, or be now influenced by, the timbre and functions of the voice. And this is Derrida's point—that "phonetic" and "non-phonetic" describe local elements within writing systems that have always and everywhere mixed the two.

Even hieroglyphics, the most famously "scriptural" system of them all, used phonograms (signs marking sound values) in addition to pictograms and ideograms or logograms (where the sign represents an idea). Since there is no visual difference between phonograms and logograms (and the same symbol can sometimes serve either function), and since moreover hieroglyphic script could be read from left to right, from right to left, or in vertical columns, later hieroglyphic systems included determinatives, symbols whose purpose was to indicate how, and in relation to what, other symbols should be read. It is this element of hieroglyphs that most interested Derrida, as it had earlier fascinated Freud, who compared dream work to hieroglyphic writing:

> It seems to us more appropriate to compare dreams with a system of writing than with language. In fact, the interpretation of a dream is completely analogous to the decipherment of an ancient pictographic script such as Egyptian hieroglyphics. In both cases there are certain elements which are not intended to be interpreted (or read, as the case may be), but are only designed to serve as "determinatives," that is, to establish the meaning of some other elements. (*SE* 13:176)

Christopher Johnson can help us follow Derrida's thoughts on this passage to a place where the nature and spacing of writing are thoroughly reconceived. Johnson begins by remarking that Freud does not imagine the content of the dream to be "somehow present in the unconscious," simply awaiting clear decipherment. Nor is the value of the hieroglyphic analogy restricted to the visual impact and the highly coded nature of its symbols. Rather, as

Derrida pointed out in his reading of Freud's passage, the interest of the hieroglyphic system has to do with its *structure*, whereby meaning is not a matter of the immediate content of writing but of the relations, locations, processes and differences that can be established between its discrete parts—its stratification or spacing. *Can be established*, which is to say that these relations are not given. As a result, says Johnson, "not only does the dream work operate idiomatically (idiolectically)—thereby rendering redundant a fixed code of interpretation—but the dream work itself actually comes to assume an importance equal to that of the decoded content of the dream."[5] And this means that we can begin to think about writing not as something written and waiting to be deciphered on the surface of the world, or as something that is exhausted by its own visual impact, but as *process* that is activated "idiomatically" (that is, uniquely, according to local conditions) at each of the moments and places where it may be said to occur.

Spacing thus seems to be a singularly promising area in which to explore the non-phonetic elements of even alphabetical writing. And it is a topic that always fascinated Derrida, who used the term as one of the series of semi-synonyms that famously organize his thought: "différance," "arche-writing," "writing," "articulation," "supplement," "trace," "breaching," "hymen," "pharmakon," "tympan," "parergon" . . . The list is much longer than it is usually said to be since in Derrida's hands any word could be made to display its own "différantial" structure, and so perform the work of deconstruction: "aphorism," "travel," "specter," "hospitality," "my," "chance," "yes" . . . Critics looking to privilege a single term have usually chosen "différance," and with good reason, for it is the most obviously theoretical of the terms and coined for its purpose rather than borrowed from a different argument. But "spacing," whose generality is absolute, for nothing *is* that is not spaced (which would be another way of saying that nothing simply *is*), works just as well, and its use spans the entirety of Derrida's writing career. It already plays a significant role in *Grammatology* and "Freud and the Scene of Writing"—in the former it is fully coterminous with "différance," while in the latter it refers to the stratification of time and space within our perceptual apparatus, where it functions to suggest both that nothing occurs punctually at a single time or in one place and that, because the visual and oral components of language cohabit and run interference with each other, they are subject to a stratification too complex for empirical consciousness to grasp.

By the middle of his career Derrida had come to identify spacing as "the first word of any deconstruction"—both the first thing to say about deconstruction and the minimal operation of deconstruction at work in everything that happens. In *Radical Atheism* Martin Hägglund elaborates the consequence of this "keyword," suggesting that an address to the problem of time (to the fact that "every now passes away as soon as it comes to be and must therefore be inscribed as a trace in order to be at all") opens "the most consistent way to defend the rigor" of deconstructive logic.[6] Hägglund uses Derrida's own very difficult early definition of spacing to insist on the "radical" nature of that logic: "In constituting itself, in dividing itself dynamically, this interval is what we might call *spacing*, the becoming-space of time or the becoming-time of space (*temporalization)*. And it is this constitution of the present, as an 'originary' and irreducibly nonsimple (and therefore, *stricto sensu* nonoriginary) synthesis of marks that I propose to call arche-writing, arche-trace, or *différance*" (*MP* 13).[7]

As I sometimes say to my students, if we can just understand this passage—or even if we have understood the difficulties in understanding it—we will know more about Derrida than most. It is easy enough to grasp that the spacing of time, from which nothing is exempt, makes it impossible for anything simply to be, in itself, because it must survive across time, which changes everything at every moment. We might even understand that it is only the *trace* (the retention of the past and the protention or anticipation of the future) that shelters and allows for the appearance of the present; this is what Derrida calls "the becoming-space of time," (and if we note that it is what we might call *an archiving of time that produces the present*, we will be well positioned to encounter the complexity of Derrida's later thought about the archive). But the second half of the formula, "the becoming-time of space" (which is, Derrida always insists, "co-implicated" in "the becoming-space of time"), is harder to get hold of, for it requires us to accept that space is not a volume or room or something to be filled but more like a hologram, a picture formed when a light beam is split in the presence of an object and its parts redirected onto a recording medium, from which the resulting patterns of interference can be reconstructed as a three-dimensional photograph. If time is spaced, even space, it seems, is on a timer! Or as Hägglund explains, "the spatial inscription can archive time and thus make it possible to grasp alteration, but it is itself exposed to alteration at every juncture."[8]

Already in *Grammatology*, spacing was the term Derrida used to describe the cross-fertilization of "the becoming space of time and the becoming time of space" that renders the present an "irreducibly non-simple . . . synthesis of marks." But there was a period following its publication, still early in his career, when Derrida toyed with spacing in a more restricted and material sense, an enterprise in which he was aided by typographers such as Dominique de Fleurian, the layout artist who worked with him on *Glas*, and Richard Eckersley, whose designs for the English translation of *Glas* and *Cinders* added powerful visceral weight to the argument that space and time were always already split by each other. Strictly speaking, this demonstration was not necessary, and it is possible that Derrida came to regret both the time it had taken him (for the works in question were produced using not a computer but typewriter, scissors, and glue) and the misunderstandings to which it laid him open.[9] For if the burden of *espacement* is that every moment must be recorded in order to be, but every inscription is open to alteration at every moment, that is nothing more or less than Derrida's own expanded definition of writing. And if spacing were something that *could* be illustrated, then any instance of writing would do. But the truth is that if arche-writing can be thought about and processed through a series of metaphors, it cannot, for obvious reasons, be shown.

Nevertheless, beginning with *Dissemination* (1972), which focused the question in relation to Mallarmé's own theory and practice of what he called *espacement*, Derrida undertook a series of provocative experiments with fonts and layout evident in such works as "Tympan" (the introduction to *Margins of Philosophy* [1972]), *Glas* (1974), "Living On—Border Lines" (1979), *Cinders* (1982), and *The Truth in Painting* (1987). A fragment from *Glas* reads like a paragraph from a Situationist manifesto (and so seems familiar in its attempt to be strange): "Let us space. The art of the text is the air it causes to circulate between its screens. The chainings are invisible, everything seems improvised or juxtaposed. This text adduces by agglutinating rather than by demonstrating, by coupling and decoupling, gluing and ungluing, rather than by exhibiting the continuous and analogical, instructive, suffocating necessity of a discursive rhetoric" (*G* 75b).

Elsewhere Derrida worked with more circumspection. Barbara Johnson, who translated *Dissemination* into English, describes the visual appearance within that volume of Derrida's essay on Mallarmé:

> One of the first things to notice about "The Double Session" is its provocative use of typographic spacing. From the insertion of *Mimique* into an L-shaped quotation from Plato to the quotations in boxes, the passage from *Un coup de dés* and *Le Livre*, the reproduction of Mallarmé's handwriting, and the pages bottom-heavy with footnotes, it is clear that an effort is being made to call the reader's attention to the syntactical function of spacing in the act of reading. Through such supplementary syntactical effects, Derrida duplicates and analyzes the ways in which Mallarmé's texts mime their own articulation, include their own blank spaces among their referents, and deploy themselves consistently with one fold too many or too few to be accounted for by a reading that would seek only the text's "message" or "meaning."[10]

Johnson is usefully precise here, and her precision is worth further specification. She says that Derrida is drawing attention to the syntactical function of spaces (that is, here, to their part in making writing legible); that he follows Mallarmé in miming the "articulation" of a text (that is, the creation and the joining of verbal units and the regulation of the spaces between them); that Derrida's spaces "duplicate" and "analyze" that which, in Mallarmé's work, is already a "mimicry" of meaning; and that he analyzes the ways in which Mallarmé undermines our sense of reference by deliberately confusing the issue as to what is "inside," and what is "outside" a literary text. This particular indecision is what Derrida means by the "fold." In his preface Mallarmé explains it by saying that "the paper intervenes each time as an image of itself," and we could explain it by saying that he intends it to be both the signifier and the signified "paper."[11]

These claims are modest, and perhaps only the last is "deconstructive" in the sense that it has been pushed by Derrida to the point where it becomes a new thought. But others have found in the fractured and teeming pages of Derrida's midcareer something that can be taken as a justification for their own desire to promote the visual appearance of writing as a counter-charm to logocentrism. "Inscription alone," Derrida once said, rashly, "has the power of poetry, in other words has the power to arouse speech from its slumber as sign" (*WD* 12). This formulation is certainly misleading, but even here Derrida is *not* saying that inscription is a type of language that, "deceased as a sign signal," has somehow come into its own *as what it is*. Rather, his argument is that inscription, which (unlike speech) emancipates sense from the context of its first performance, is never heavy with itself or with a truth it won't reveal; on the contrary, it is light, feckless, moveable. The passage continues: "writing creates meaning by consigning speech, by entrusting to an engraving, a groove, a relief, to a surface, *a mark whose essential characteristic is to be infinitely transmissible*" (*WD* 12, translation modified, emphasis added). The word inscription conjures up ideas of stony permanence, but you can see that Derrida is not suggesting that writing "enregisters" meaning or anything else once and for all; on the contrary, it puts both the mark and its meanings into play and throws them toward an illimitable set of future contexts. If something strange is here apprehended about the visual sign, it is something that is going to demand of us rigorous, rather than magical, thought.[12]

Derrida's decision to use typography to enhance or stage the meaning of his own text was hardly innovative. In fact, it wasn't new for Mallarmé, although *Un coup de dés* so impressed his contemporaries that his claim to be the originator of such experiments is now widespread. If venerable and sacred visual writing practices such as Islamic calligraphy and Hebraic "micrography" had little significant influence on the concrete poetry and visible language experiments of the late nineteenth- and early twentieth-century European avant-garde, the use of "visual" writing in commerce, to attract the eye of potential customers, is itself traditional.[13] So when Derrida's texts appear to aspire to be the image of what they would express—when, for example, he allows himself to say that the asymmetrical x that is a figure for chiasmus "can always, hastily, be thought of as the thematic drawing of dissemination" (*TP* 166), or when the English translators of his essay on Valerio Adami say for Derrida that the original "was printed in eighteen point type, without margin, border, or passe-partout of any kind. And is primarily concerned to explain this fact"—we are being invited to play a very old game. It is scarcely philosophy, it is more like squinting, for it asks you to *look at* rather than abstract meaning from writing—or, rather, since this is too easy, to look at and read a text simultaneously (*TP* 150). Like trying to drive wearing bifocals while consulting a map (or, be it said, like trying to read *Glas* for the first time when, Derrida imagines, you might want to "protest against the strabismus that someone wants to inflict on you"), the experience is uncomfortable (*G* 114b). But when twentieth-century artists claimed to have found forms of writing that could overturn the "tyranny" of philological and semantic conventions—when Kandinsky admired "poetry that has not been smothered by the meaning of the word," and when Derrida used his own *mis-en-page* to draw attention to the visual appearance of writing and so escape the "suffocating necessity of a discursive rhetoric"—this is what is being asked of us (*G* 75b).[14]

This effect arises not where writing is visible (most writing in the narrow sense is that), but when we don't know what to do with it. Should we try to *read* it, or will we look like fools or mystics if we do? Are we perhaps being asked to apprehend a special value, something at play in the space between seeing and reading and more than the sum of its parts? "The setting out of the lines requires to be followed with the eye, as well as the contents with the mind," says Dickens's Thomas Sapsea, "purest Jackass in Cloisterham," while, appealing to Jasper's judgment as a man of taste, he hands him the vain and inappropriate inscription he has commissioned for his wife's tomb. Following Dickens's own instructions, which specify the placement of large, small, and very small capitals, editions of *Edwin Drood* usually reproduce the banal typographical extravagance of Sapsea's vision so that readers can see it for themselves, feel for Jasper's embarrassment at being asked to approve the setting and the sentiment, and share his relief when he manages an unexceptionable response: "Impossible not to approve. Striking, characteristic, and complete."[15]

But if Jasper's reply appeases the widower's vanity, it notably fails to address the relation between the "setting" and "meaning" of the lines. This relation is extremely difficult to grasp: faced with +R+, or with *Glas*, most of us can do no more than agree with Thomas Sapsea that the setting out of the lines requires to be followed with the eye, as well as the contents with the mind, while noting in addition that these itineraries do not run on identical paths. As Derrida said himself, considering the relation between the discourse of *Glas* and its reappearance as a fractured script within one of Adami's drawings, "a rebel to . . . the regulated exchange of the two elements, close to piercing a hole in the *arthron* of discursive writing and representational painting, is this not a wild, almost unnarratable event" (*TP* 160)?

Almost unnarratable? Is the event of this relation narratable or not narratable? It is Derrida's deliberate failure to answer this crucial question that keeps him safe while leaving the rest of us exposed to the lure of tame reading.[16] And it is this very crisis—for there is no meaning without "the setting out of the lines," and also no meaning *in* their setting out—that Derrida found staged in Mallarmé's writing, where he called it the "re-mark." The example on which he and Mallarmé both focus is the word "*blanc*" ("white," "blank," "space"), which has so many semantic associations and is used so often in *Un coup de dés* that, Derrida says, readers become sensitized to the presence of a term that "permeates his entire text, as if by symbolic magnetization." Furthermore,

> the white also marks, through the intermediary of the white page, the place of writing of these "whites"; and first of all the spacing between the different significations (that of white among others), *the spacing of reading* . . . The white of the spacing has no determinate meaning, it does not simply belong to the plurivalence of all the other whites. More than or less than the polysemic series, a loss or an excess of meaning, it folds up the text towards itself and at each moment points out the place ("where nothing will have taken place except the place" [*Un coup de dés* 474–75]), the condition, the labor, the rhythm. As the page *folds in* upon itself, one will never be able to decide if *white* signifies something, or signifies only, or in addition, the space of writing itself. The use of the word *pli* ("fold") and its variations (*pliage*, *ploiement*, *repli*, *reploiement*, etc.), which is as frequent, produces the same effects. (M 115–16).

"The white/blanc of the spacing has no determinate meaning," says Derrida; it is not the symbol of absence, nor the picture of a space, nor a sign of things that cannot be said. The white that is white space is not written or otherwise presented; rather, it is the site of the occurrence of the word "blanc." Which means that neither word nor substrate are in a simple place, for the white that is "pointed out" by the white paper obviously cannot be where the word "white" is written (a place which is white no longer). For the white to appear as such, marked as a "white," there has to be displacement. Derrida's point, truncated here and difficult to grasp, is that it is not the blank space on its own but *the blank space working with the word blank* that "points out the place 'where nothing will have taken place except the place.'"

Typographers have long known that rigorous dealings with writing quickly bring you to a place where meaning reveals itself to be dependent on the place, conditions, rhythms, and orders (that is, speaking locally, the spaces, organization, and syntax) of the matter that supports it. Typography is predicated on the assumption that what is cognized is structured by bibliographical formats, as well as by the physiological and cognitive aptitudes of readers, before the apprehension of textual content begins. If it does not and cannot speak (nor even, in the narrow sense, write) about the matter, it silently posits the existence of a kind of apprehension that, not merely somatic, not only emotional, and not yet linguistic, is nevertheless the precondition for our response to language. The interest of typography for Derrida, and its consequence to the project of cultural graphology, surely lie in the fact that it "points out" an experience of cognition best understood not as a *representation* of the world to the person who perceives it but rather as an ongoing bringing-forth of the world through a process of living in and through the dynamic organization of its spatial archives.

Since *everything is spaced* there would be something bathetic or even mistaken about trying to track the operations of *espacement* in written texts per se. We cannot expect to see "the becoming space of time and the becoming time of space" pictured, as it were, in print work ("the truth in painting," as Derrida titles his collection of four long essays on visual art, only to reveal, of course, that that truth concerns its own "irreducibly non-simple" synthesis of marks). And my brief here is modest: it is only to bring into focus some of the non-phonetic elements of our writing system. Nevertheless, in selecting sixteenth-century type ornament for this focus I have found myself sliding towards a place of temptation—for we are dealing with a topic whose study can leave you feeling that you have seen something very like (although it is safer to call it something that is merely about) espacement.

Deconstruction must neither reframe nor dream of the pure and simple absence of the frame. These two apparently contradictory gestures are the very ones—and they are systematically indissociable—of *what* is here deconstructed.
«Derrida, *The Truth in Painting*, 73»

In the middle of the sixteenth century European printers began to experiment with the use of ordinary, moveable types, each of which carried not a letter, but a decorative element. Used individually, as "single spot" designs such as the asterisk, the hedera (vine leaf), or the Maltese cross, such ornaments had been used to mark divisions in writing long before printing began; and even as type ornaments they are almost as old printing itself. But in the 1550s French and Italian printers started using types with individual design elements that, put side by side like the letters of a word, composed themselves into serial patterns.[17] The results were electrifying. A single set of ornamental types could now be combined into a number of different designs, while if two or more sets were used together further patterns emerged (see figure 1).

In 1819 the inventor of the kaleidoscope, David Brewster, claimed that its capacity to produce art through the inversion, multiplication, and varied combination of a few simple forms allowed it "to assume the character of the highest class of machinery," for it not only "abridges the exertions of individuals" but also outdoes "the operations of human skill" in the production of the beautiful.[18] Before the invention of photography, which Walter Benjamin identified as constituting a break line in the history of the function of art, the kaleidoscope appeared as an optical apparatus that depended on a market and breached the "aura" of the art object. But the same can be observed, and observed earlier still, in relation to type ornament, whose compositor is amanuensis both to the market and to a mechanical process for which no human operator can be solely responsible. Even the craftsman who designed and perhaps cut the punches that made the matrices out of which a set of ornamental types was cast could not anticipate the multitude of individual designs that might result from their composition with others (as Derrida said in a different context, "the otherwise of the 'and so on' then becomes my theme" [*TP* 193]).[19] The allure of such designs, which could be used to make borders and ornaments of any size and shape, was felt immediately, and within a few years of their introduction combined ornamental fonts were being used by printers across Europe.[20]

This fascinating phenomenon has not been much studied. Historians of the book have recognized that when it first appeared

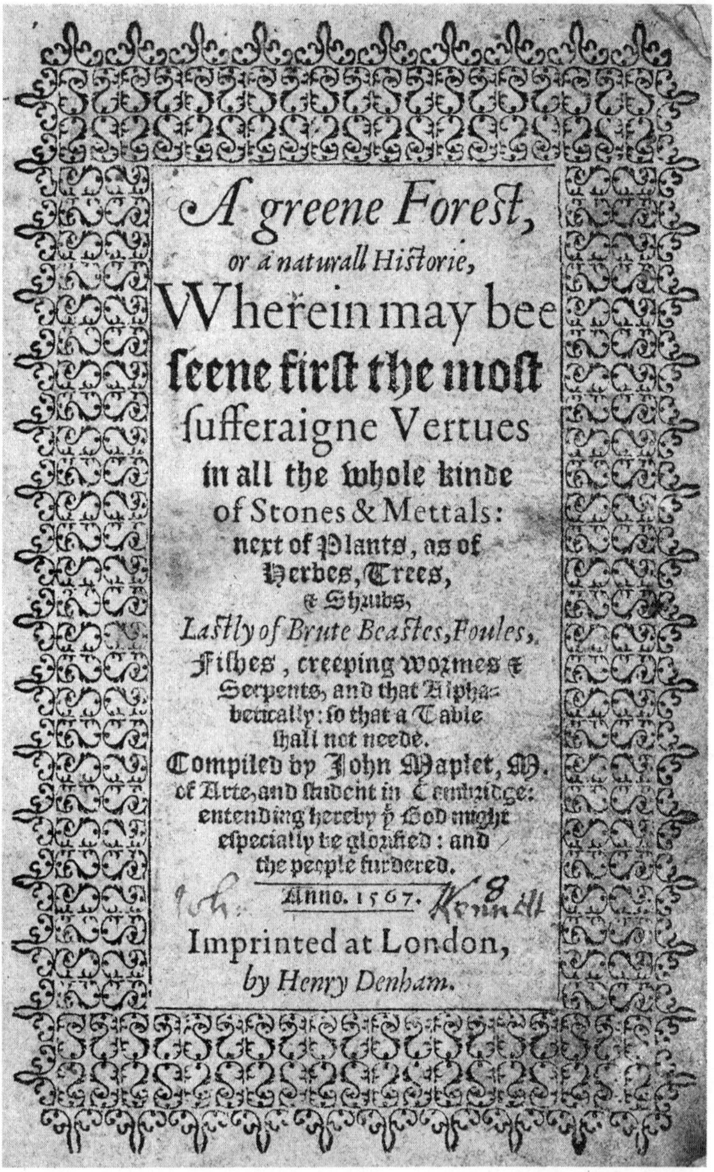

A greene Forest,
or a naturall Historie,
Wherein may bee
seene first the most
sufferaigne Vertues
in all the whole kinde
of Stones & Mettals:
next of Plants, as of
Herbes, Trees,
& Shrubs,
Lastly of Brute Beastes, Foules,
Fishes, creeping wormes &
Serpents, and that Alpha-
betically: so that a Table
shall not neede.
Compiled by John Maplet, M.
of Arte, and student in Cambridge:
entending hereby y^t God might
especially be glorified: and
the people furdered.
Anno. 1567.
Imprinted at London,
by Henry Denham.

1. Frontispiece composed of three different ornamental types for John Maplet, *A Greene Forest* (London: Henry Denham, 1567). Denham, one of the first English printers to embrace type ornament, used these types so frequently that they became a signature of his work.

type ornament was a visual innovation that spoke to the new optical and cognitive work of reading a printed page, and they have suggested that its purpose was to give readers more familiar with manuscripts some approximation of the ornamented pages they had been used to when they now opened a printed book.[21] They have proposed that type ornament worked to "rest the eye," or "focus the concentration," to reward readers with an experience of the beautiful, and even, since type ornaments are also called flowers, "to remind us in the artifact of the natural world around us."[22] I have proposed elsewhere, as additional reasons for its popularity with printers, that it supported the paper and so helped keep pages flat and unsmudged during printing; that it was used to mark divisions and articulate continuities within printed texts; and that it could also be deployed, albeit in fleeting and unsystematic ways, to mark the work of individual print shops, as the signature of individual authors or of coteries, and to identify texts as belonging to particular genres or kinds.[23]

Each of these purposes could also have been met using other kinds of ornament. The unique feature of type ornament is that it allows an exploration and celebration of the intellectual and cognitive resources of the specific technology that is moveable type. It does this by looking as much like printed writing as it is possible to look without actually being it. Type ornament thus "re-marks" the novelty of type as an event in the visual field, drawing attention to its size and shapes, its characteristic weighting of black lines against a white field, its composition from the combination of individual but uniform letters, and to the fact that, if not limitless, it continues much longer than the eye can see, through many pages and multiple copies, always outpacing our need.[24]

Those with experience designing and setting type have themselves stressed the compatibility between letters and ornamental types. William Addison Dwiggins praised the Caslon ornamental designs as constituting "a true flowering of the letter forms . . . as though particular groups of words had been told off for special ornamental duty, and had blossomed at command into intricate, but always typographical patterns." Francis Meynell and Stanley Morison also found type ornament to be "most letter-like in feeling, in balance, and in 'colour,'" and they proposed that each unit could be considered as a "letter" in "the language of decoration" that can be composed by a capable printer "into words, into sentences, nay into poems or proclamations of that mysterious language."[25]

Typographers are remarkable for the pleasure they take in what they do; but others have shared their sense that type ornament comprises an inscrutable script that may be more meaningful than one that can be read: in the late nineteenth century the Baconian controversialist Harold Bayley began to feel that he could see Rosicrucian symbols "woven with subtle ingenuity" into certain books by means of their type ornaments (see figure 2).[26]

In the sixteenth century, when anyone who had the money was surely tempted, at least once in their lives, to buy a book on the grounds that *it had printed writing in it*, type ornament must have helped to sell books. Strips of type ornament survive with surprising frequency printed on the "A" page of English books that contain the same designs on their internal pages (see figures 3 and 4). Printed as part of the first sheet of the first quire, the "A" page functioned as a paper cover to protect the title page of an assembled but unbound book; whatever had been printed on it was dispensable and designed to be discarded when the book was bound, but before that it provided a way to identify unbound volumes as they lay for sale on a stationer's stall. And here the type ornament, printed in a script that, saying nothing, seems to promise everything that *could* be said, works to advertise printed writing as a determinate product that could satisfy indeterminate wants: "Look! A book with printed writing in it. It could be the very one I need . . . ."

Type ornament, in other words, offered its first customers a pleasurably intensified encounter with printed writing such as could scarcely be experienced by reading it. But the fact that type ornament is a facsimile (from Latin meaning "made alike") of writing has been obscured by the names under which it has been known. The earliest English term, which is also used for any border with a running or trailing design, is "*vinet*" or "*hole vinet*."[27]

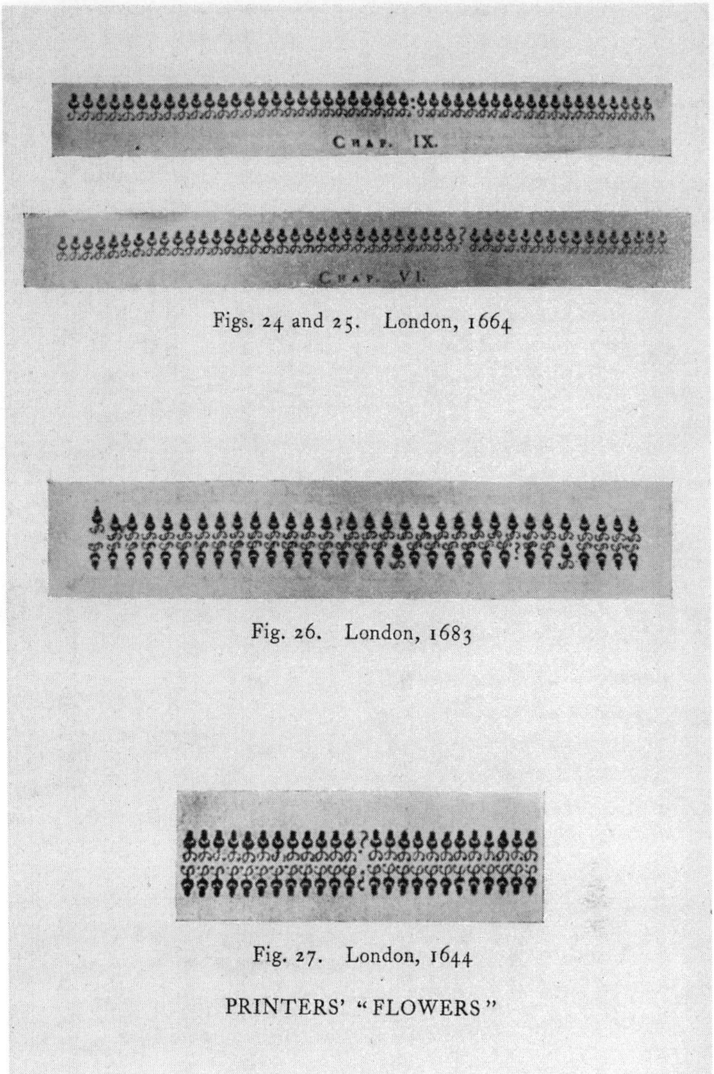

2. Early twentieth-century plate showing specimens of mid-seventeenth century "single spot" flowers, in which Harold Bayley believed he saw the Rosicrucian symbols of rose and fleur-de-lys.

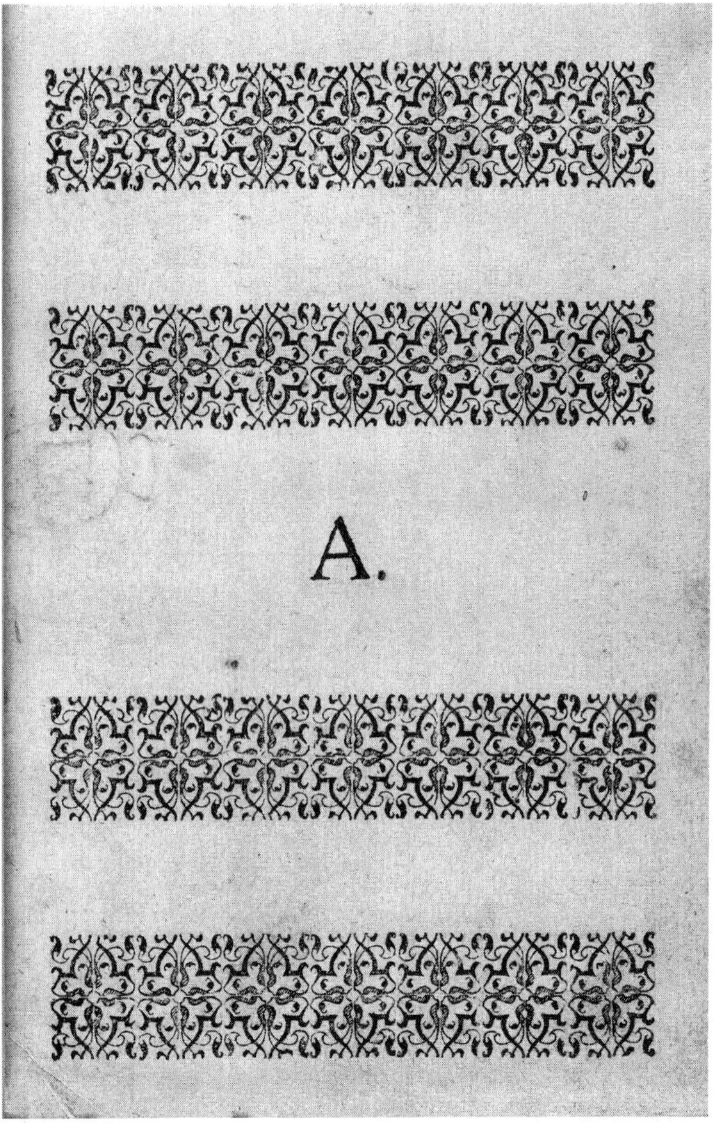

A.

3. "A" page from *Greene's Funeralls* (London: John Danter, 1594), showing strips of the same type ornament used within the volume.

Doubtless, we could enhance our sense of the original purpose and impact of type ornament—that it could be used to fill difficult or narrow spaces and to hide structural supports, and that it is so easily multiplied as to become invasive—if we now called it printers' vines, and remembered that the *hedera*, or Aldine leaf, is an ivy that once wreathed the text blocks of medieval pages. Reappearing in the new medium of print as the single spot design of the Aldine leaf, it is only waiting for the opportunity to spread again.

Type ornament has also been called printers' lace, an apt name for the designs produced in the sixteenth-century. For these were almost without exception in the Europeanized "arabesque" style referred to in England as "rebeske" or "branched work," a late, westernized version of the interlaced, foliated patterns whose use had been perfected in the Islamic countries of the East by the twelfth century.[28] The invasion of Spain from North Africa and the later establishment of trading between Constantinople and Venice in the fifteenth century brought these designs to Europe, where they were disseminated on carpets, cloth, pottery, book bindings, and metal goods (the original "damask ware").[29] The motifs of such work ultimately derive from the imitation of plant forms, but its characteristics are the abstraction and stylization of these forms, the rhythmic effect of their repetition, and the fact that none of the component elements of the design can dominate the whole or appear to be marked for attention.[30]

In the second quarter of the sixteenth century a series of printed pattern books became available that further recast these designs to make them more useful for European craftsmen (metalworkers, ceramicists, weavers, lace-makers, embroiderers, and others).[31] Flattened into two dimensions, deprived of their original architectural or religious consequence, and reproduced in collections that indiscriminately mixed different local styles, these "arabesque" motifs were easily believed, in the sixteenth century as later in the nineteenth, to be "destitute of natural symbolism and of ideal signification," a belief supported by the understanding that Islamic art had developed its abstract patterns in response to the Koran's injunction against figural representation.[32]

From the position of her considerable familiarity with early modern books Katherine F. Pantzer observed that around 1635 type ornaments changed from "large and relatively lacy designs" (that is, from the interlaced arabesques of vinet, which were often composed several lines deep, or even into whole fields) to "blacker, blunter, and usually smaller designs"—that is, to single "spot" motifs that could be arranged in rows but not composed into continual running designs (see figure 2).[33] These later designs, which are usually referred to as printers' flowers, were often representational and could be used, as one early historian put it, "in a manner germane to the subject matter of the work," as when death's heads decorate a funeral sermon, or crowns and thistles punctuate a political pamphlet. But the "lacy" designs of sixteenth-century type ornament resist such iconic use. Free of semantic associations, they appear on the page as a particularly pure form of writing in its non-phonetic aspect.

And before we get to flowers there is more to think about lace. So much, in fact, as to make you wonder why we have been so long content to use weaving as the dominant metaphor for writing.[34] Of course the word "text" claims a root with "*textus*" (a tissue) from "*texere*" (to weave), an association authorized by Quintilian, who used it to refer to oral composition and intended it to suggest, as it does rather well, that a text is something more than the sum of its parts, and exists as the play of tension between them. But few among us now have seen a loom, or know how to set one up, and the metaphor has come to be used to refer to the *act* of writing, as if its essence concerned making something in a craft setting. If this seems a small step, the difference between writing as a play of tension and writing as the local production of a textual object is large—indeed, it is the terrain on which Derrida erected the whole of *Grammatology*.

In any case, the metaphor of weaving has been worked to death: "weaving is a textual process," says Robert Scholes, "the creation of a textile or web out of mere threads," and the best image for an English teacher is as "an instructor of textuality, a weaver of texts who teaches such weaving to others."[35] As the metaphor of weaving is wearing thin, the manufacture of other textiles is sometimes used to figure writing: spinning, sewing, embroidering, even felting has been tried . . . but at some point our confidence fails, and few have proposed tacking, tackling, crochet, netting or making samplers as useful metaphors for writing. Except Derrida. "If text means tissue," he noted, then the essays comprising *Writing and Difference* have been "roughly basted": within and between them things are not woven together or neatly sewn up but tacked in place so as to retain their potential to be differently configured (*WD* ix). In 1975 he regretted not having used the resources of the term *cramponnement*—hooking, clinging, or hanging onto something ("it's quite a word, don't you think?")—to address the issue of attachment in *Glas* (Pt. 5). In 1982, giving the lecture that would become "Mes Chances," he remarked that his lecture would amount to "loosely woven netting" aimed at an audience in a way "somewhat analogous to fishing or hunting" (MC 2); and in 1998 he anticipated that his work on Jean-Luc Nancy would amount to "no more than a sampler, more or less well-sewn" (*OT* 138).

The truth is that you can't read very far anywhere in Derrida's work without being brought up short by a consideration of how the fabric of things holds or fails to hold together. Hooking, tacking, netting, lacing, appliqué, the insert, the patch—Derrida considers what each of these reveal about the contingency of discursive forms (including those of speech; after all, the work of the Greek rhapsode was to *stitch songs together*). Even weaving is transformed in his hands (or perhaps we should say the metaphor is returned, in all its useful strangeness, to Quintilian), for here the threads that make up a text systematically fail to hold each other permanently in place *for essential reasons*:

> Whether in the order of spoken or written discourse, no element can function as a sign without referring to another element which itself is not simply present. This interweaving results in each "element"—phoneme or grapheme—being constituted on the basis of a trace within it of the other elements of the chain or system. This interweaving, this textile, is the text produced only in the transformation of another text. Nothing, neither among the elements nor within the

system, is anywhere ever simply present or absent. There are only, everywhere, differences and traces of traces. (*Po* 26)

One day we must begin the search for a textile metaphor that reveals the costs as well as the benefits of writing as a mode of production that occurs on an industrial scale: polyester, perhaps, that Arcadian-sounding, petroleum-based tissue that is the staple of one of the world's most polluting industries—wouldn't the processes of its manufacture have things to tell us about writing? Talk about dissemination! In *Glas* Derrida notes that his own "mistrust" of the textile metaphor arises from the fact that even if you are imagining something as complex and flocculated as fleece "it still keeps . . . a kind of virtue of naturality, primordiality, cleanliness [*proprieté*]." It is because sewing (*couture*) "supervenes on an artifact," and is therefore less "natural, primordial, and proper" (*TP* 208b), because it "compels reckoning with the insert, the patch" (*TP* 118b), and "exhibits what it should hide, dissumulacras what it signals," that he prefers it to weaving (*G* 209b).

For my current purposes there is no need to go to polymerization, for lace, "a net-like ornamental openwork of thread," is already a sufficiently provocative model with which to explore the values of printed writing.[36] Since its whole point is to appear both costly and unnecessary, lace immediately raises the question of worth: Why take the time to make it? Why bother with a fabric that, far from protecting us from cold or injury, requires that *we* look after *it?* Falsely modest, retiring (it won't push itself forward, its business is with cuffs and borders), lace imposes a heavy duty of care on those who own it. That it is dislikeable, a burden we put on ourselves or others, is demonstrated in Elizabeth Gaskell's *Cranford*, where shabby-genteel Mrs. Forrester preserves her lace collar, too valuable to be entrusted to her maid, by washing it herself in a preparation of milk. One day the cat, who knows the proper use of things, is caught gulping from the saucer, and the lace is only retrieved after the administration of tartar emetic—"we soaked it and soaked it, and spread it on a lavender-bush in the sun before I could touch it again, even to put it in milk. But now your ladyship would never guess that it had been in pussy's inside."[37] Now, everything that permits the progress of lace through the stomach of a cat (that it takes up little space when wet, that it needs special care, that its fragile filaments are multiplied into a monstrous durability) can be attributed to the fact that it is nothing but a regulated series of gaps and holes, a labor of time hooked and put on display. Its properties clarified from its passage through Gaskell's novel, lace emerges from the cat's throat as a provocative model for (although certainly only a phantasm of) *espacement*.

In his *Manual of Historic Ornament* Richard Glazier noted that among the decorative arts "lace is peculiar in that the production of ornament and fabric is simultaneous and inseparable."[38] Nothing but ornament, self-embellished, it is the vocation of lace to be all border, edging without a field, all edge and without edge; it can go on, and it can go on playing this game with you, repeating itself in every place and in every scale, long after you have tired of it. A sublime craft! And a strong case of what Derrida investigates under the term "parergon," the trait or framing line that spaces itself out between the inside and the outside, and is readily split because already split (*TP* 11–13). You might wonder if the logic of lace is not even stronger and more binding than that of the parergon, for if the latter indicates *what is incomprehensible about the edge*, in lace what is incomprehensible is also *at the edge*, and always prepared to multiply and so outrun us. As Derrida said himself, exhausted by the attempt to account for an exhibition of Gérard Titus-Carmel's work titled *The Pocket Size Tlingit Coffin and the 61 Ensuing Drawings*, "things always get complicated when the structure of a serial interlace [*entrelacs*] comes into play" (*TP* 202).[39] Lace suggests that the framing line is not just a question of internal divisions but that it is also space seeking, poised to overflow itself, its vocation to expand forever.

So much for lace! Can flowers be made to yield as much? For the most successful name for type ornament, the one it was given when the first accounts of its use were written in the seventeenth century and has since gained wide acceptance, is of course "printers' flowers." A term that, in its willful compression of nature and machine, seems to have been designed to provoke the old philosophical question of what a flower is.[40]

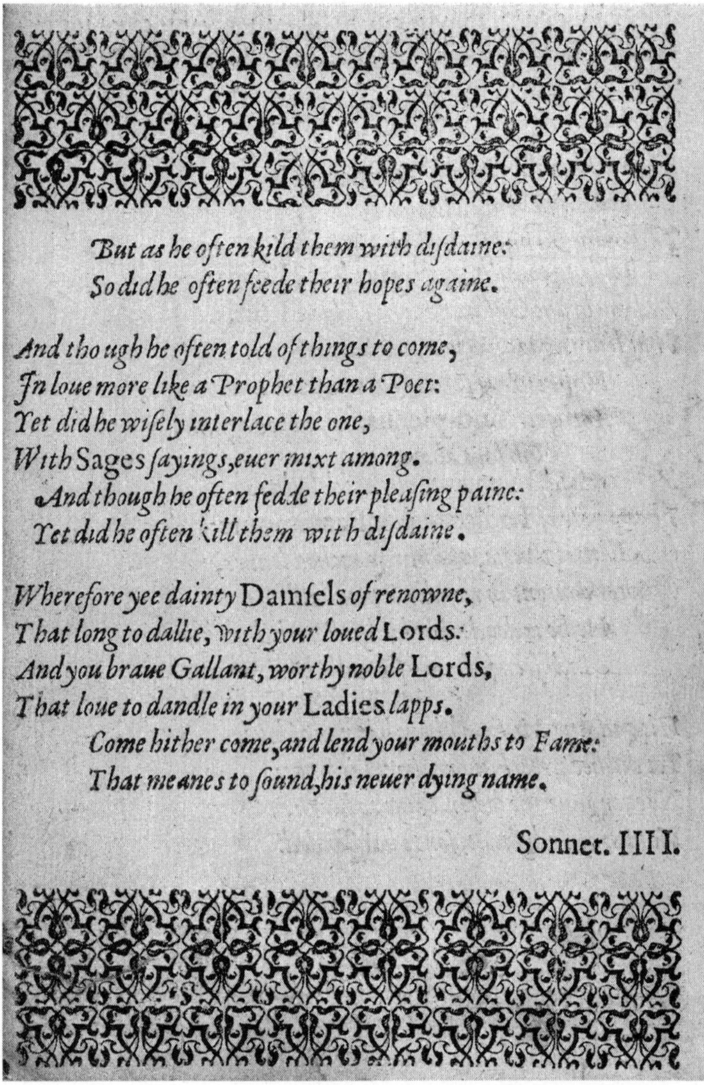

But as he often kild them with diſdaine:
So did he often feede their hopes againe.

And though he often told of things to come,
In loue more like a Prophet than a Poet:
Yet did he wiſely interlace the one,
With Sages *ſayings, euer mixt among.*
And though he often fedde their pleaſing paine:
Yet did he often kill them with diſdaine.

Wherefore yee dainty Damſels *of renowne,*
That long to dallie, with your loued Lords:
And you braue Gallant, worthy noble Lords,
That loue to dandle in your Ladies *lapps.*
Come hither come, and lend your mouths to Fame:
That meanes to ſound, his neuer dying name.

Sonnet. IIII.

4. *Greene's Funeralls* (London: John Danter, 1594), sig. B1v., interior page showing type ornament.

In *Glas* Derrida obsessively asks himself "the question of the flower," the same question in many parts, none of which can be answered. "Why say 'flowers of rhetoric'? And what would the flower be when it becomes merely one of the 'flowers of rhetoric'" (*G* 13b)? Why is the flower the "poetic object par excellence," and what is poetry, if that is so? "What is rhetoric, if the flower (of rhetoric) is the figure of figures and the place of places?" "Why does the flower dominate all the places to which it nonetheless belongs?" "Why does it stop belonging to the series of bodies or objects of which it forms a part?" (*G* 14b) Perhaps these questions cannot be answered because they already mean that the flower cannot be read. "Are you going to fall precipitously into the trap," Derrida asks himself (and others), and claim to know what flowers are doing in Genet's work? Are you going, for example, to claim that the flower, "which signifies (symbolizes, metaphorizes, metonomizes, and so on) the phallus," gets "caught in the syntax of the cuttable–culpable," and so "signifies death, decapitation, decollation"? The language of flowers is always willful, "Anthologos signifying the signifier signifying castration" (*G* 27b–28b).

It is certainly tempting to look at some sixteenth-century English books and see flowers there—even flowers used "in a manner germane to the subject matter of the work." It is not uncommon to find pocket size prayer books and other "manuals" set within skeleton frames, whereby the text block on every page is surrounded by type or other ornament (one reason for this is that the ornament protects the text as the edges of the tiny book get worn away in use). These frames were so commonly used for prayer books as to function almost as a generic marker for them—to own such a book is already to move towards prayer; you might say that the ornament marks an intention to pray, or even (what might be much the same thing), that it is a prayer itself. John Conway's *Meditations and praiers*, for example, was set in 1569 by its first printer Henry Wykes within frames of type ornament that so dominate the text as to raise the question, not easily answered, as to whether they are part of the work or extraneous to it (see figure 5). Certainly the decision of Conway's printers to retain the scheme, recomposed each

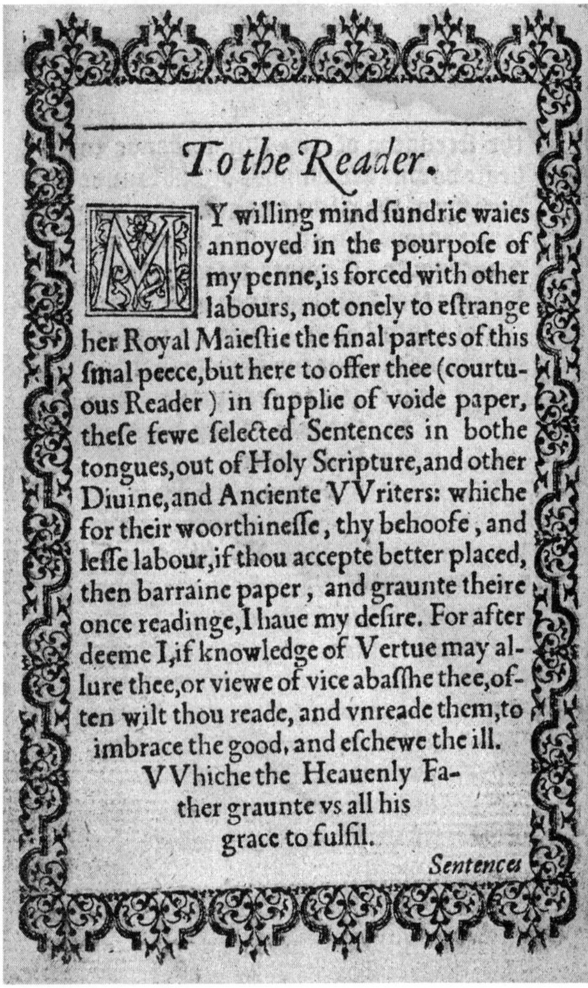

To the Reader.

MY willing mind ſundrie waies annoyed in the pourpoſe of my penne,is forced with other labours, not onely to eſtrange her Royal Maieſtie the final partes of this ſmal peece,but here to offer thee (courtuous Reader) in ſupplie of voide paper, theſe fewe ſelected Sentences in bothe tongues,out of Holy Scripture,and other Diuine,and Anciente VVriters: whiche for their woorthineſſe, thy behoofe, and leſſe labour,if thou accepte better placed, then barraine paper, and graunte theire once readinge,I haue my deſire. For after deeme I,if knowledge of Vertue may allure thee,or viewe of vice abaſſhe thee,often wilt thou reade, and vnreade them,to imbrace the good, and eſchewe the ill.

VVhiche the Heauenly Father graunte vs all his grace to fulfil.

Sentences

5. Internal page from the first edition of John Conway's *Meditations and praiers, gathered out of the sacred letters, and virtuous writers: disposed in the fourme of the alphabet of the queene majesties name. Whereunto are added comfortable consolations* (London: H[enry] Wykes,1569).

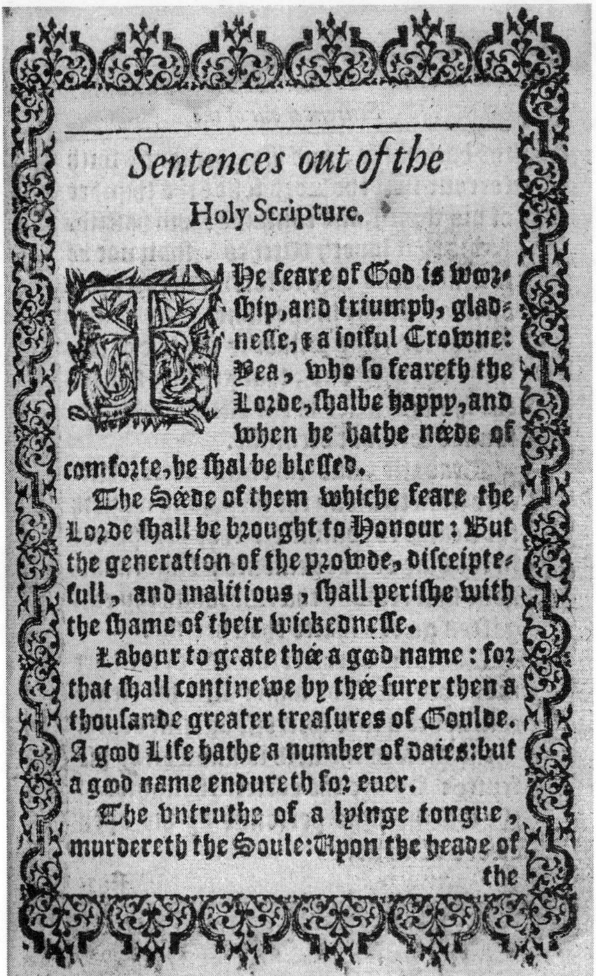
Sentences out of the
Holy Scripture.

THe feare of God is worship, and triumph, gladnesse, & a ioiful Crowne: Yea, who so feareth the Lorde, shalbe happy, and when he hathe neede of comforte, he shal be blessed.

The Seede of them whiche feare the Lorde shall be brought to Honour: But the generation of the prowde, disceiptefull, and malitious, shall perishe with the shame of their wickednesse.

Labour to geate thee a good name: for that shall continewe by thee surer then a thousande greater treasures of Goulde. A good Life hathe a number of daies: but a good name endureth for euer.

The vntruthe of a lyinge tongue, murdereth the Soule: Vpon the heade of the

5. (continued)

time in different flowers, suggests that they felt the type ornament was a prominent or expected feature of the work—perhaps even its best part.

In the final edition, published in 1611, eight years after Conway's death, the running headline, "The poesie of floured prayers," has become the main title and the contents have significantly changed. The book is now dedicated to Princess Elizabeth, daughter of James I, rather than to the old Queen, who had died in 1604, and the acrostic prayers that repeatedly spelled out the word REGINA have been replaced with those spelling LADY.[41] That this is not judged a new work can be attributed, at least in part, to its retention of the ostentatious setting of the earlier editions, and suggests that the layout of a text is sometimes a larger part of its identity than we are ready to admit (see figure 6). Here the situation is intensified by the fact that the skeleton frame has served as if it were a mold into which words were poured, or as a structure with a moveable base that lets now one thing, and now another, appear.

But if the old subtitle and new title of this repurposed book indicates that it is a florilegium or gathering of "flowers," that is because "flower" means an excellent rhetorical trope or figure such as could be collected with others to form a "posy" of poetry. "Flowred" also suggests something refined or sifted, for flour is the best part, the "flower," of the wheat (such is the origin of the term "flour"). Conway's posy of flowered prayers is thus a choice selection of beauties whose excellence is "re-marked" by the heavy use of type ornament. It is concerned not with flowers as they grow in the field, nor with flour as it is refined by bolting, but with flowers as they serve as a metaphor for that which is selected and noted as being at the height of excellence. A text that knows all this no longer knows what a flower is.[42]

The flower is one of the typical passions of the human spirit. One
of the wheels of its contrivance. One of its routine metaphors.
One of the involutions, the characteristic obsessions, of that spirit.
Let's change our minds about it.
Outside this involucrum: The *concept* which it became

> By some devolutive revolution, Let us return it, safe from all definition, to *what it is.*—But what, then?—Quite obviously: a *conceptacle.*
> —Francis Ponge, *Changed Opinion as to Flowers* (*TP* 103)

Inset without comment into "Parergon," an essay in which Derrida reads Kant's *Critique of Judgment* as constituted and flawed by the gesture with which it frames the beautiful, this passage from Ponge proposes that we will never be free to see the flower *as it is* because we can relieve it of the concepts with which it is burdened only by putting others in their place. Ponge judges the substance of Kant's claim, that we find flowers beautiful *when and because they mean nothing*, to be impossible. "Flowers are free beauties of nature," Kant had argued. "Hardly anyone but a botanist knows the true nature of a flower, and even he, while recognizing in the flower the reproductive organ of the plant, pays no attention to this natural end when using his taste to judge of its beauty" (*CJ* 72).

According to Kant, to find a flower beautiful a botanist has only to disable his knowledge of its purpose until representing nothing, "no Object under a definite concept," it appears to him in the guise of unattached beauty (*CJ* 72). But not just anything is beautiful: to give rise to a judgment of beauty a thing has to be organized *as if* toward a purposive end. What is "freely" or purely beautiful would be, as Derrida puts it, "any finalized organization not signifying anything, not representing anything." Such organized forms can also show or signify things, as the flower does when a botanist regards it with a professional eye, but they are free beauties only by not doing so, only "insofar as *somewhere they apply themselves or bend themselves to not doing so*" (*TP* 97, emphasis added). In Kant's scheme free beauty must be somehow re-marked as being *out of use.*

But already (and this is Ponge's point) it seems impossible not to have thoughts about a thing that requires us to be indifferent as to whether it exists or not. You or I might imagine a souvenir whose long survival has rendered its purpose mysterious, so that the tending of its form towards some end is wrapped in melancholy. Derrida, less sentimental but scarcely more detached,

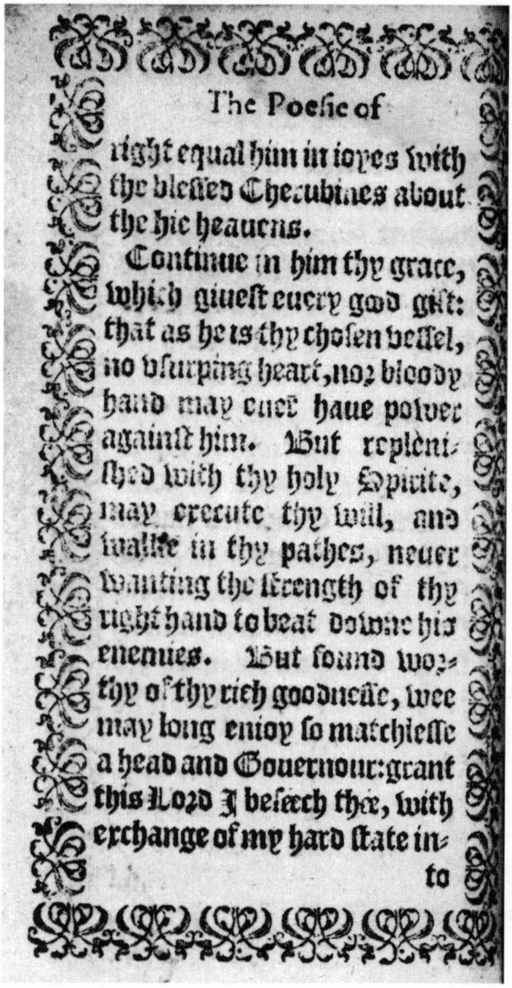

The Poesie of

right equal him in ioyes with the blessed Cherubines about the hie heauens.

Continue in him thy grace, which giuest euery good gift: that as he is thy chosen vessel, no vsurping heart, nor bloody hand may euer haue power against him. But replenished with thy holy Spirite, may execute thy will, and walke in thy pathes, neuer wanting the strength of thy right hand to beat downe his enemies. But found worthy of thy rich goodnesse, wee may long enioy so matchlesse a head and Gouernour: grant this Lord I beseech thee, with exchange of my hard state into

6. Internal page from the fourth, posthumous edition of John Conway's *Meditations and praiers* (London: Edward White for Valentine Sims, 1611). Retitled *The Poesie of Floured Prayers* and containing re-purposed text, this edition (like the second and third) reproduces the skeleton frame of the first using a different font of type ornament.

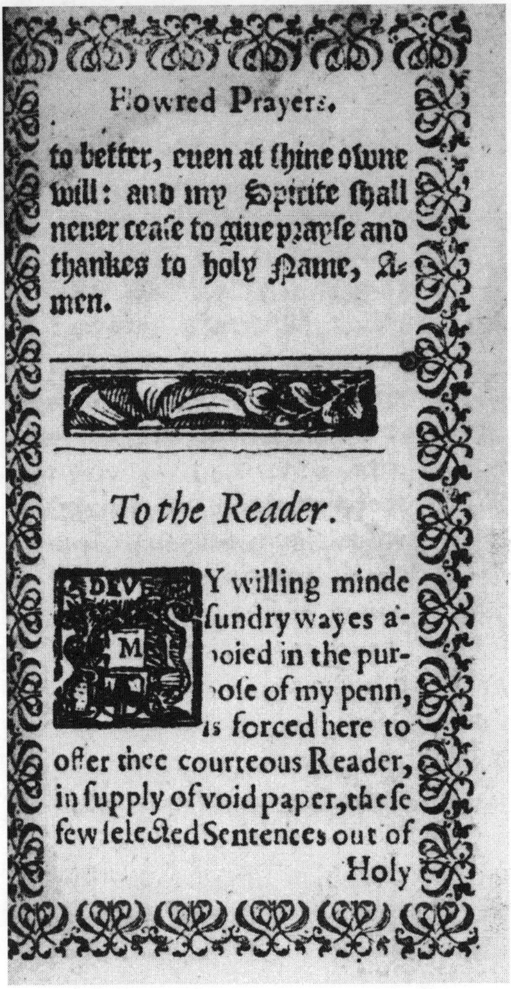

Flowred Prayers.

to better, euen at thine owne will: and my Spirite ſhall neuer ceaſe to giue prayſe and thankes to holy Name, Amen.

To the Reader.

MY willing minde ſundry wayes annoied in the purpoſe of my penn, is forced here to offer thee courteous Reader, in ſupply of void paper, theſe few ſelected Sentences out of Holy

6. (continued)

pictures with deliberate clinical violence the blow that severs the object from its purpose—this is what he calls, in a phrase that evokes blood as well as deprivation, "the *sans* of the pure cut" (*TP* 82–118). The point is that neither you nor I nor Derrida will agree with Kant that the interruption of purpose that produces a beautiful object can ever be clean. The *sans* of the pure cut is Derrida's way of acknowledging, as Kant does not, that "such a pure and disinterested pleasure . . . determines the judgment of taste [as] *the enigma of the bereaved relation—labor of mourning broached in advance—to beauty*" (*TP* 44, emphasis added). For Derrida this relation reintroduces the concept *completeness-incompleteness*, "and a concept always furnishes a supplement of adherence. It comes at least to stitch back up again, it teaches us how to sew" (*TP* 94).

Within the provoking list of things that Kant says man finds "freely" beautiful are exotic birds, such as parrots and hummingbirds; "a number of crustacea"; "music that is not set to words"; and "designs á la grecque, foliage for framework or on wall-papers, etc." Such things, he finds, "have no intrinsic meaning; they represent nothing—no Object under a definite concept—and are free beauties" (*CJ* 72). You might think, as Derrida notes, that the frame of a picture could often and easily be judged to be freely beautiful (*TP* 97). You might think, as he does not note, that this is precisely what the inclusion of "foliage for framework [*Laubwerk zu Einfassungen*]" on Kant's list is meant to suggest. But in fact Kant had already put the frame in its place, along with the charm of colors and the agreeable tone of musical instruments, as adjuncts whose business is only to make the form of what each augments "more clearly, definitely, and completely intuitable." And "if the ornamentation does not itself enter into the composition of the beautiful form—if it is introduced like a gold frame merely to win approval for the picture by means of its charm—it is then called finery [*Schmuck*] and takes away from the genuine beauty" (*CJ* 68; *TP* 53).

You can see the problem (it is the one at which Derrida's entire reading of the third *Critique* is aimed): Flowers be hanged—we don't know what a frame is.

Derrida has exhaustively made this point.[43] It is not only the argument that governs all four essays that comprise *The Truth in Painting* and his work elsewhere on titles and signature; before any of this, it was already what was at stake in his early and infamous statement in *Grammatology* that "il n'y a pas d'hors-texte [there is nothing outside the text]"—a claim we should now elaborate to include the proposition that the text is not on the outside of being, to which it then points or refers, but *being as its own outside*. If Derrida identifies moments like Kant's invocation of gilded or foliated frames as "a sort of incoherence-effect," "an embarrassment or a suspended indecision in the functioning of the discourse," (*TP* 115), these are only local instances of the inexorable logic of the parergon, the bane of philosophical analysis, the baffling principle whereby the line that marks the inside from the outside "comes against, besides, and in addition to" the work but does not simply "fall to one side," for "it touches and co-operates within the operation from a certain outside." "Like an accessory that one is obliged to welcome on the border, on board [*au bord, a bord*]," as Derrida puts it in a series of untranslatable puns, "*It is first of all the all aboard* [*Il est d'abord l'a-bord*]" (*TP* 54, translation modified and emphasis added).

But this quality, while strange, is also familiar (if it were not, it would scarcely be worth the attention that Derrida gives it). In fact, it is what William Addison Dwiggins was pointing to when he described the Caslon ornamental types as a detachment from the rest of the font:

> Excellent as single spots, the Caslon flowers multiply their beauties when composed in bands or borders as ornamentation for letterpress. They then become a true flowering of the letter-forms—as though particular groups of words had been told off for special ornamental duty, and had blossomed at command into intricate, but always typographical, patterns.

Told or counted off, like soldiers on assignment, the ornamental types are a detachment of letters assigned to represent the whole of which they are a part, and from the other members of which they differ only in having been so delegated. "Detachment," muses

Derrida in *Glas*, "the cutting, deliason [*déliason*], to be sure, but also the representative delegation, the sending of a detachment, on a mission close by the other, close by self" (*G* 98b).

To understand type ornament in this way is to be able to see the printed page not as site for information but as a visual field whose intricate black lines and white spaces provoke sensations of movement and light and whose vibrating surface combines regularity and recurrence with a commitment to systemic local variance. Making the visual proposition "this is what writing looks like" even as it continues to manifest its own isotropic beauty, type ornament encourages readers to think about writing under the aspect of appearance, and by turning the page into nonpurposive space it breaks the stranglehold that the semantic function otherwise exerts over phonetic writing. "Thus, in (the) place of the flower, the anthographic, marginal and paraphing text: which no longer signifies" (*G* 30b).

Still, it is worth remarking that, to the untrained eye of most readers, type letters and type ornament do not stay combined but separate like a poorly made mayonnaise. It is even true to say that the decorative and the semantic elements are never *seen* together (even where, in a well-formed letter, they are the same thing). For where text is read, its beauties will be overlooked; and where its beauties are studied, the text disappears. Perhaps this is what type ornament is set to teach, for if you are a reluctant reader, you can banish printed words by studying their forms: now the page is a site from which you can gather conceptual information, now it is a visual field without semantic content, now it is telling you something you want to resist, now it is an abstract pattern whose vibrating network of black lines and white spaces provoke sensations of movement and light. Having so far forgotten yourself in the pleasures of the game, you will be able to feel what Derrida meant when he spoke about "the condition, the labor, the rhythm" of writing in Mallarmé's work; and you will begin to see leading figures in the script and in the letter forms: stairways to climb, paths and rivers down which you can travel, shapes to lean against, spaces in which you might hide.

Melanie Klein's young patients played this game when they exhibited some of the forms of the "distaste for learning" that she identified as inhibition:

> Seventeen-year-old Lisa related in her associations that she did not like the letter "i," it was a silly jumping boy who always laughed, who was not needed in the world at all and over whom she became quite enraged . . . She praised the letter "a" as being serious and dignified, it impressed her . . . Then she thought that "a" was, perhaps, a little too serious and should have at least something of the skipping "i" . . . Nine-year-old Grete associated with the curve of the letter "u" the curve in which she saw little boys urinate. She had a special preference for drawing beautiful scrolls that proved in her case to be parts of the male genitals—Lisa for the same reason omitted flourishes everywhere. (*LGR* 66)

But *who* is inhibited—those who can't read because they see in the script the engaging figures of their own psychic histories, or those like me and you, who think they just want to read? Centuries before modernist poets and painters sought to free themselves from the "tyranny" of semantic meaning, printers' flowers were quietly effecting the same revolution, transforming the printed page into a site for the release of our fantasies and for the enjoyment of our own projective behaviors, and reminding us that the gathering of semantic meaning is only one of several cognitive responses to writing—and one that cannot distinguish for itself the demarcations between psychic, somatic, and external stimuli, or the difference between what is present to consciousness and what is re-marked, within it, as a sign.

3

Sign Tailoring

The question posed here being one of knowing whether *a* text could be *one* and if such a thing exists any more than a unicorn.
«Derrida, *Glas*, 169b»

And what of Derrida's third topic, the *becoming literary of the literal*? He glossed this as calling for "a psychoanalysis of literature that would be respectful of the *originality of the literary signifier*" where "until now, only the analysis of literary *signifieds*, that is, *non-literary* signified meanings, has been undertaken." I think he had two things in mind: First, to identify literature as a discourse that resists philosophy's desire to restore presence by erasing the signifier (in Derrida's terms such a discourse is perhaps already "literary").[1] Second, to distance himself from Lacan, whose two foundational essays "Seminar on 'The Purloined Letter'" (1955) and "The Agency of the Letter in the Unconscious or Reason Since Freud" (1957) were republished in 1966 in *Écrits*, and appeared to some, as they did to Lacan himself, to have anticipated Derrida's work.[2] Derrida's pointed response to this provocation, which was published in 1975 as "The Factor of Truth," took such close hold of Lacan's reading of Poe that Barbara Johnson later claimed she couldn't know whether the two men "were really saying the same thing, or only enacting their differences from themselves."[3]

Now, if to read is to carry some truth away from the text (but this is precisely the question that each essay debates) we would have to say that, together or apart, neither piece is fully legible. But since Derrida's essay is a focused attempt to work out a psychoanalysis of literature that would be respectful of the *originality of the literary signifier*, and since this promises to be as fruitful for the field of cultural graphology as it has already proved liberating for psychoanalysis, we can't ignore it; we are going to have to cut our own way through the thicket of opportunities that it represents. To be forced to break a path like this can be a good thing. That cutting opens and activates the text and the world and may prove to be the most consequential of the gestures that Derrida has to offer scholars of the text will be my own argument in this chapter.

Let's start at the trailhead of "Seminar on 'The Purloined Letter'" (ignoring, as we must, the paths leading back from there to Marie Bonaparte, Saussure, Freud, Poe, Kant, and others). Here Lacan used Poe's story to illustrate his argument that the repetition compulsion (which Freud had identified as an expression of the death drive) finds its basis in the *insistence* (that is, the agency, as well as the authority or dominance) of the signifier; and that the signifier, although it allows for local imaginary effects of all sorts, is finally wedded to the logic of the Symbolic chain that it serves. While the human subject imagines himself to be the author or transmitter of a signifier whose consequence depends on the meaning that it carries, in truth it is the signifier that is assigning the subject his place, in accordance with a trajectory in which its semantic burden plays no part. "You think you act," says Lacan, in the voice of the signifier, "when *I* stir *you* at the mercy of the bonds through which I knit your desires. Thus do they grow in force and multiply in objects, bringing you back to the fragmentation of your shattered childhood" (SPL 71, emphasis added).

As Lacan sees it, the signifier is filled with an uncanny power that acts on everyone who uses it, including those who resist: "the signifier determines subjects in their acts, in their destiny, in their refusals, in their blindness, in their end and in their fate . . . willingly or not, everything that might be considered the stuff of psychology, kit and caboodle, will follow the path of the signifier" (SPL 60). Lacan reads "The Purloined Letter" as an allegory of this disquieting truth, arguing that what is at stake in Poe's story is not the meaning of the letter that the Minister steals from the Queen (we never learn its contents), but the fact that whoever holds it adopts the same position as the person from whom they took it. The "frolics" of the elegant society as it passes from the Queen to the Minister to Dupin to the Chief of Police "would have no meaning," says Lacan, "if the letter itself were content with having one" (SPL 56). Lacan's position is not that the letter can have no meaning (on the contrary, it could have several) but that its function is not to be confused with them nor (and here he departs from Klein) with the "various psychical and somatic functions that serve it in the speaking subject" (*Écrits* 148).

You could be forgiven for thinking that the "Seminar on 'The Purloined Letter'" met Derrida's criteria for a psychoanalytic criticism committed to the *originality of the literary signifier*. Lacan thought so, and even Derrida conceded that such work put him well in advance of Freud or any of his followers in its readiness to encounter the formal and material organization of the signifier (PT 43–44, 45).[4] But you can also see the problems coming: The apparently small differences that Derrida will erect into the towering problems that allow him to say that Lacan's way of doing things is not what he is after, not at all.

The first of these concerns literature. While Lacan speaks in illuminating ways about the signifier, using Poe's fiction to illustrate his point, he has not, says Derrida, taken full account of the fact that his signifier is operating in a *literary* setting, which stages the action in an "abyssal structure where it no longer belongs to the realm of decidable truth" (PT 88). The problem is not that Poe's action is invented but that (at least for Derrida, although he is scarcely alone in this) literature—and in particular a fiction like "The Purloined Letter"—is a discourse whose identifying feature is that it resists being reduced to the illustration of a discoverable truth, be it a general law (say, of psychoanalysis), or a more local "real" event. And if he has avoided an obviously semantic or thematic analysis of the text, Lacan has nevertheless read "The Purloined Letter" as an allegory of the truth of castration, analyzing the "displacement of the signifier" (its circulation, and the fact that it is "never in its place") as if it were the signified content of the story.

That Derrida, in bringing this charge against Lacan, was guilty of finding his own truth in a particular fiction was not lost on Barbara Johnson, who ended her long and brilliant essay on their engagement by admonishing them both that "what is un-decidable is not certain things, but whether a thing is decidable or not."[5] Like a mother imposing peace on her sons, Johnson judged them to be equally at fault. She read them more carefully than they read each other, and she may be right. But you can imagine the younger child squirming at the injustice, for as *he* would see it the certain thing that Lacan finds in Poe's story is the single truth of castration, whereas the certain thing for Derrida is that a literary text has *no* decidable truth—and this for formal reasons that can be explained. You are glad that Johnson packed them both off, you would have liked to have done it yourself, but you can sympathize with an indignant young voice coming back from wherever it has been sequestered: "but I am *not* as bad as him! My *point* is that to claim writing as the truth in literature is, above all, not to make a truth claim . . ."

Derrida's second reason for distrusting Lacan's analysis has to do with the ways in which, according to Lacan, the signifier makes its presence known. Why does it *speak?* "You think you act when I stir you at the mercy of the bonds through which I knit your desires . . . So be it: such will be your feast until the return of the stone guest I shall be for you since you call me forth" (SPL 71). Although Derrida does not do so, we might ask, in addition, why the signifier speaks *like this*, in the voice of Molière's Commendatore, the outraged father whose statue, suddenly and horribly alive, calls Don Giovanni to his final reckoning: "You invited me, and I have come . . . the hour of your doom is arrived."[6] Most statues, when driven to speak, take a similar tone: "'My name is Ozymandias, king of kings: Look on my works, ye Mighty, and despair!'" But we are used to thinking that these are just stories and that they represent either the bombast of the narcissist who ordered the statue ("You can't see the ambition of a dead man go further than this," says Molière's Don Juan, when he first sees the tomb of his enemy), or the paranoid fantasies of the passers-by, perhaps ourselves, who believe the stone has addressed them. Is Lacan *serious* in suggesting, on the contrary, that in the voice of the statue we hear the ring of truth?

From his first writings Lacan showed himself heir to a particularly strong form of phonocentrism: "speech is the key," he said in 'The Agency of the Letter,' and today psychoanalysis "must find in speech alone its instrument, its context, its material, and even the background noise of its uncertainties" (*Écrits* 147). But the hyperbole of the statement already indicates that we are dealing with a speech that has been dislocated from its traditions—this is not speech as communication between people that may or may not fail, nor even speech used to disguise thought from ourselves and others. What is worth pointing out, says Lacan, is another function of language, one we know nothing about, when it signifies "something quite other than what it says," which is "the place of the subject" (*Écrits* 155). It is because the subject does not know this place, or that he is in it, that the signifier marks the site of our reduction "to the state of blindness that is man's in relation to the letters on the wall that dictate his destiny" (SPL 72). Here speech is not the site of presence, but of the subject's most intimate relation to an exterior or unconscious force. And now we know why the signifier chooses that sepulchral monotone; it is because, even as speech, it originates outside the speaking subject. Another way of putting this would be to say that in the voice of the signifier we encounter speech coming back at us *as if it were writing*, its commanding power grotesquely enhanced by this double displacement.

But if, in such gestures, Lacan seems to have hold of Derrida's subsequent claim that speech is no more "present" than writing, both claim and consequences are here recomposed in strangely ruined form. After Lacan's death Derrida himself invoked the closeness of their thinking to justify the standoff between them and rebrand it as a form of love (*R* 39–69), but in "The Purveyor of Truth" he clearly holds Lacan's description of the signifier to be slightly—and therefore very dangerously—out of gear, inappropriately formulated as an uncanny voice, and wrong again when re-conceived as a doom-laden letter. "The insistence of the Lacanian letter is the sublation of writing in the system of speech," and all Lacan has managed to do is invest the letter with the uncanny power that he elsewhere gives to speech (PT 85). It was against the mystique of this power that Derrida had trained all his energies in *Grammatology*.

Derrida's third disagreement with Lacan concerns the nature of the "letter," which Lacan staged as a question of materiality. "By *letter* I designate that material support that concrete discourse borrows from language. This simple definition assumes that . . . language and its structure exist prior to the moment at which each subject . . . makes his entry into it" (*Écrits* 147–48). So it is not *very* material, this support that "concrete discourse" borrows from the structure of language; it is not a palpable thing but the differential system that Saussure called *langue*—and so far, so good. But in the "Seminar on 'The Purloined Letter'" Lacan stressed the "materiality of the signifier" differently. Describing it as "odd in many ways" he specified two particularly puzzling properties, both of which he saw exemplified in the history of the letter that circulates in Poe's story: that it will "not admit partition" and that it has a singular relation to place: "we cannot say of the purloined letter that, like other objects, it must be or not be in a particular place but that unlike them it will be and not be where it is, wherever it goes" (SPL 55). This second claim may look to be *exactly* the one that Derrida formulated for himself as différance or espacement—until you see the conclusion that Lacan draws from it: what the "purloined letter" means "is that a letter always arrives at its destination" (SPL 72).

What did Lacan intend by this? Perhaps no more than to underline the assertion Freud had sought to prove through an accumulation of examples in *The Psychopathology of Everyday Life*, that there is no chance or accident in the unconscious; that the bungled, tattered, or insulting message that arrives is the one we unconsciously wanted delivered. Lacan's own interest in linguistic errors was a product of his understanding of language as an agency that has structured us before we try to use it—which represents an advance over Freud's description of parapraxes as the product of unconscious wishes that express themselves by disrupting conscious intentions. But Derrida thought Lacan's formulation was simply wrong: "this 'unique materiality,' deduced from an indivisibility that is not found anywhere, corresponds in fact to an idealization" (PT 84). It is not empirically true, he argued, tendentiously, that if you "cut a letter in small pieces . . . it remains the letter it is," or that the "letter always arrives at its destination"; it is only "the ideality of a letter" that resists division and diversion, and continues to be itself in whatever battered material form it takes. Indeed, the proper conclusions to draw from Poe's short story, thought Derrida, and even from Lacan's own reading of it, are that the letter *can always be divided* and *can always not arrive*.

Derrida returned to these propositions in "Mes Chances," first delivered as a lecture at a conference on literature and psychoanalysis in 1982. Into this work, rich as Nile mud and as playful as anything he ever wrote, he stirred Democritus, Lucretius, Heidegger, and Shakespeare (although only to quote Freud citing *Hamlet* and to regret that he had no time to conduct the reading of *King Lear* that seemed called for), while returning to Freud's *Psychopathology of Everyday Life* in order to reopen his argument with Lacan over Poe. But the essay is, from beginning to end, about chance: its interface with necessity and the fact that "its effects appear to be at once produced, multiplied, and limited by language"—including Derrida's own (MC 2). What are the chances that, as he addresses his audiences, his message will be received and understood? Better than if he had not spoken or written at all, and yet compromised by the enormous reserves of indetermination which are what allow the signifier to be applied in different local circumstances.

And what is chance? Perhaps it can be thought of as the interruption of a dispatch or trajectory without which nothing would happen at all, the *clinamen* or unmotivated swerve in falling "atoms" (*littera*, literally "letters") that, according to Lucretius, produced clusters of matter and thus gave birth "to the worlds and things they contain" (MC 7). But having invoked this Epicurean doctrine Derrida rejects what he calls the "*atomistique*" of the proposition that *littera* are irreducible elements. And here he sharpens his difference with Lacan, arguing that if the axiom that the letter resists partition allows Lacan to track the letter in Poe's story as it moves on its determined course, and therefore to say what that literary text is "about," it is also the cause of his limitation as a reader. For there is, says Derrida, no understanding literary fiction ("not to mention of what I call writing or the trace in general") unless you can face up to "a certain divisibility or internal difference of the so-called ultimate element (*stoikheion*, trait, letter, seminal mark). I prefer to call this element (which, precisely, is no longer elementary and indivisible) a *mark*" (MC 10).

I think it is fair to say that at this crossing of psychoanalysis, literature, and the *mark* we are at the tightly fused center of Derrida's early thought—and at a nodal point for the development of cultural graphology. But what is the relation of this chance-inflected, divisible element (we might call it *the mark that swerves*) to literature? Let's make sure we understand what Derrida calls the *essential insignificance* of the mark—and how it differs from the "odd" materiality of Lacan's letter. First, the mark, which is what is called trace or arche-writing in *Grammatology*, is not necessarily a verbal sign but extends beyond human language; another way of saying this is that language is only one among several informational systems that run on marked elements. Second, *as concerns the system of language*, a mark must be capable of being repeated and recognized as the same from one context to another. Derrida called this iterability *grafting* and argued that it was already writing: "To write means to graft" (*D* 355). It is iterability that gives linguistic marks what appears to be an ideal identity and, "since one associates indestructibility with indivisibility," the impression of an irreducible solidity (MC 16). But this is a chimera, for "the identity of such a mark is *also* its difference and its differential relation, varying each time according to context, to the network of other marks." The "ideal iterability" that makes a mark a mark, by releasing it from one context to play a part in another, also ensures that the mark has no identity, "because by means of this essential insignificance the . . . ideal identity of each mark (which is only a differential function without an ontological basis) can continue to divide itself and to give rise to the proliferation of other ideal identities" (MC 16). Which is to say that writing as grafting proceeds without a rootstock—"the graft is not something that happens to the properness of the thing. *There is no more any thing than there is any text*" (*D* 355, emphasis added).

In brief, Derrida's argument is that the letter as mark is divided before it sets off and further divided and therefore diverted on impact, and that literary fiction allows us to trace, as in a cloud chamber, the determinations, diversions, and chances of the letter in the effects of these divisions and combinations. For if the literary text situates marks to look like the play of solid entities, it does not let us forget the precariousness of the contextual circumscription that allows for this appearance. Furthermore, even as it serves as the frame and medium that allows us to understand the seriousness and consequence of its own determined but chance-led division, the literary text is *itself* a singular but recombinant mark. As Derrida writes: literary "oeuvres befall us. They speak about or unveil that which befalls *in* its befalling upon us" (MC 17).

That literature is a question of framing within which individual works are "re-marked" as such has been argued by others, although never perhaps as exhaustively as by Derrida himself. Less familiar, and certainly less worked over, is his striking proposition that the cause of the frame and the source of the re-mark is fission: "My *clinamen*, my luck, or my chances (*mes chances*) are what led me to think of the *clinamen* beginning with the divisibility of the mark" (MC 16).

Once you have learned to see it, the figure of cutting or division is everywhere in Derrida's writing. Perhaps it begins with his consideration of *breaching* (*Bahnung*, path-breaking, the cutting or opening of a conducting path in the psychic apparatus) in "Freud and the Scene of Writing." From there it moves through *Dissemination* (1972), where Derrida elaborates what Phillip Sollers identifies as *scission*, the violent, arbitrary cut of beginning; to *Glas* (1977), where division is intensified into a principle of mincing or "morselling"; to *The Truth in Painting* (1978), where each of the first three essays meditates on some aspect of detachment, while the last worries Heidegger's account of Van Gogh's painting "Old Shoes with Laces" with the question "To whom and to what are we to restitute, to reattach?" (*TP* 259). From then on Derrida had the cut at his disposal as a gesture and as a thesis. If "there were one and only one deconstruction," he noted in *Resistances of Psychoanalysis* (1996), "a sole thesis of 'Deconstruction,' it would pose divisibility: différance as divisibility" (*R* 33).

It is important to stress différance here, as it will protect us from falling into the "atomistique" of Lacan, Lucretius, and any theory of culture that is predicated on the identity of indivisible units. As Derrida sees it, analysis will never get us down to pure elements or entities, and *it is because there is no end to division that analysis is both possible and interminable.* "Divisibility, dissociability, and thus the impossibility of arresting an analysis, like the necessity of thinking the possibility of this indefiniteness, would be perhaps, if one insisted on such a thing, the truth without truth of deconstruction" (*R* 33–34).

All the same, in Derrida's writing division has different moods. In *Circumfession* (1991) he positioned circumcision as the cut that severs the circle of the same. "Bad as this may seem," argued John Caputo, "this cut is not a loss but a gain. For by preventing the closure of the signature, the cut provides an opportunity to discover, to invent, to come upon (*invenir*) something new, the coming of the other, yes, to the incoming of the other" (*DN* 198). Caputo nicely captures the mood of what I want to call the positivity of cutting, which represents Derrida's official line on the matter. Why not be optimistic? If everything is already sectioned, and divisible, it seems we have little to fear from the special form of unbinding that is the cut (except perhaps the forces of rebinding that are immediately unleashed).

But when Derrida mobilizes the cut in a local setting, when, as it were, he invites us to see it in the flesh, I think it is true to say he has a tendency to flinch. In *Archive Fever* circumcision is not protected from anxiety about the knife. Proposing that the dedication written by Freud's father on the flyleaf of the family Bible that he had just had rebound for his son's thirty-fifth birthday also commemorates Sigmund's circumcision, Derrida notes that under the pressure of "the pellicular superimposition of these cutaneous marks . . . each layer seems to gape slightly, as the lips of a wound" (*AF* 22). And earlier, in *Dissemination*, both Derrida and Sollers find that castration, and therefore loss, is "always at stake" in the scissions they otherwise celebrate. As the pen turns into a knife both their texts become littered with images of severed heads, mutilated genitals, gashes, and bleeding edges—Derrida's third section, "The Scission," is awash with blood (*D* 300–306).

Drawing its destructive energies from the writings of Genet, *Glas* is even more explicit about the violence of its own "morselling," which it also relates to castration, while Derrida's reading of Adami's portrait of Walter Benjamin in *The Truth in Painting* (an essay that picks up some of what *Glas* left off) is darker still, for if castration is a price we pay for access to the law, here the cut yields no compensation. "Why de-tail [*de-tailler* or cut out]? For whom [*pour qui*]?" asks Derrida in relation to Adami's tendency to "detail extracts." And having claimed that "picking out the enlarged detail comes . . . from cinematographic and psychoanalytical technique," he can still find only the gloomiest answer: Adami's details mark the place of what has disappeared (*TP* 175–81). Benjamin's empty glasses, his famous downward-looking pose, and his name are selected by the artist to commemorate the man without cenotaph (*TP* 178). Inventoried in this way, Benjamin's effects have the power to suggest that it was precisely details—names, addresses, and further particulars—that allowed him and others to be picked out by the machines of genocide.

But if within psychoanalysis the cut always refers back to castration, so that even circumcision cannot easily be thought without wincing, this rule is not binding everywhere; and, whatever Derrida says, "picking out the enlarged detail" is *not* a technique that is special to psychoanalysis or the genocidal bureaucracies of the twentieth century. It is not even special to cinematography. Rather, it is what *everyone* does when they write or read (from the Latin *lego*, *legere* meaning to gather or pluck). "What causes writing," he observes in *Glas* in a passage that deserves to be more celebrated, "is what separates [*écarte*] and sows [*sème*], scatters [*essaime*], sign-cutting and sign-sewing [*signacoupure et signacouture*]. What desingularizes, unseals, desiglums, opens the eyes by blinding" (*G* 171b). The cut, we might say, is the différantial origin of writing that brings signs into being, forges connections ("desingularizes"), opens the text, enlarges on its details ("desiglums"), helps us see. Furthermore, if cutting has its moods, it is also true that a change of tone or mood is also a cut, a rerouting, a chance to see things differently.

"Why de-tail [*de-tailler* or cut out]?" (*TP* 181). *Why?* How can we not? Certainly that is how *Glas* is assembled, from clippings of Hegel and Genet ("I cut into the 'complete works,' I tailor [*taille*] another text there") (*G* 17b). But you don't have to be Derrida to read or write in this way—everybody does it. Indeed, there is no reading (and no writing, therefore no arche-writing, and therefore no living) without cutting. This, of course, is Derrida's own point: "what affords reading affords reading by citations, necessarily truncated clippings [*coupures*], repetitions, suctions, sections, suspensions, selections, stitchings [*coutures*], scarrings, grafts." Thus does one text encroach on or "become infatuated" with another, says Derrida, and if all this "does not happen without profit or loss to the organism that undergoes grafting," we will never be in a position to adjudicate between the sum totals of what has been lost or gained (*G* 168b).

But for scholars at least it can be easier to count what gets lost in the graft. Which may be why, although we have long been familiar with the processes of material cutting and stitching that produced manuscripts, we have not wanted to notice that early modern readers cut as they read, and read by cutting, printed books. Over the centuries librarians and archivists have preserved and described manuscripts into which printed matter had been sewn, stuck, or interleaved, as well as printed books with extensive manuscript commentaries and annotations into which manuscript pages had sometimes been added; and they have also identified and named "hybrid" books, of which it cannot not be said with confidence whether they are printed books with manuscript additions or manuscript books with printed additions. But catalogue descriptions of these volumes suggest that, in many cases, those who wrote the entries struggled not only with a lack of agreed terms to describe what they saw but also against their own disapproval of it. My class was once shocked and impressed when one of its members arrived with a detachment of loose pages that, torn from her hard copy, comprised the week's reading of *Grammatology*, and it must be a rare archivist who can regard a sixteenth-century hybrid book as an embellished manuscript, without regretting the now rare volumes that were sacrificed in its making.

Perhaps the most obvious practical benefit of Derrida's work on cutting is that it allows us to question the assumptions with which, as textual scholars and as critics, we have hitherto gone about our business: that each printed book is a totality, whose ideal form is somehow established at the end of the production process, beyond which point it can only be compromised by further material alteration, and that the printed book is the best stronghold for the information it contains. A finished book magically prohibits the thought that its contents might be better appreciated and used, and perhaps even better preserved, outside the protection of hard covers. To be able to entertain such thoughts, to understand why Derrida called the first chapter of *Grammatology* "The End of the Book and the Beginning of Writing," is to be in a position to recover the activities and assumptions of some early modern owners as they read—that is, cut and adapted to local circumstances—their own books.

For as the books themselves demonstrate, early-modern readers cut and pasted printed matter for a variety of unexceptionable reasons: to remove proscribed or offensive material from prayer books and primers, to obviate the labor of copying in producing commonplace books and other compilations, to reformat texts in order to rationalize the material they contained, to provide room for marginal or other commentaries, to add other material to and thereby expand a given text, to organize their own researches, and to illustrate or embellish presentation and other manuscripts with motifs cut from printed sources. Such cutting should be understood not only as a work of grammar (properly understood, as the organization of written information), but also as an act of writing.[7]

The cut opens, gathers and sorts; it shapes the present and introduces the future. No wonder it has moods, and no wonder these are various. But let's emphasize the positive, the Derridean optimism, unflinching for the moment. Cutting marks for attention elements that may be permanently overlooked (and therefore improperly stored) at their original sites, and preserves what will otherwise be lost to the accidents of time and historical indifference. It takes images and other formulations whose mass production or overuse has led to their exhaustion, and it brings them back to life by putting them outside the circuits of commodity production. It clears the mind and the air and the vision, opening new possibilities for the future. And even in its sharper guise the cut can be an injury that frees. *Virescit Vulnere Virtus*, says the motto adorning a pruning knife in the emblem on the central panel of what are now known as the Marian hangings—"Virtue flourishes by wounding," or, as we might say, "injury strengthens the worthy," or even "strength comes from cutting" (figure 7). Embroidered by or for Mary Stuart during the years she spent under house arrest with the Earl and Countess of Shrewsbury, the emblem is sometimes read as expressing a wish that the barren Tudor line be cut back so that a fruitful branch of the Stuarts could flourish in its place. If, as is reported, Mary sent an earlier version of the scheme to the Duke of Norfolk, she may have in-

7. Portion of the bed hanging worked by Elizabeth Talbot, Countess of Shrewsbury, and Mary, Queen of Scots, England, 1570–85 showing a hand with a pruning knife and the motto "Virescit Vulnere Virtus."

tended as much. But the motto, like the sentiment, is ancient; and the Biblical reference that it engages and relates to the vine suggests a loving discipline rather than the cutting back of rivals: "I am the true vine and my Father is the Husbandman. Every branch in me that beareth not fruit he taketh away; and every branch that beareth fruit he purgeth [prunes] it, that it may bring forth more fruit" (John 15: 1–2). And this is best gardening practice—correct pruning does not just remove the barren and the dead but also cuts the fruitful branch that it may flourish still more.

How can literary scholars think about the cut as that which promotes new growth? To pose the question like this is already to answer it. Really, we just need to stop thinking in wholes. What, after all, would be a whole tree or vine? At what point would we need to stop its growth and seal it off from the environment from which it draws its life and from the parents and ancestors from which it takes form in order to say that such and only such is its whole and proper body and state? (Here you can be reminded of the usefulness of Derrida's claim that "il n'y pas d'hors texte," by which he meant, as we have already seen, not that there is no real world but that any text is so embedded in the world that there is no way of extricating it without "carrying off at the same time an unformed mass of roots, soil, and sediments of all sorts," and no way of reading it that does not graft it into and onto foreign soil (*Grammatology* 161).

If it can be granted that cutting is an unexceptional method of information management and can be a useful and sometimes felicitous discipline even to the entity cut, it has still to be shown what this has to do with literature. In 2004 Adam Smyth, noting that the early modern practice of inserting, pasting, or binding printed pages within manuscripts had been largely overlooked by scholars, constructed an impressive exception to this rule with his description of the miscellany book of Sir John Gibson, compiled while he was in prison for debt between 1655 and 1670.[8] This quarto volume contains a wide diversity of entries in English, Latin, and Greek. Those in manuscript include sermons, poems, transcriptions from the Bible and the Book of Common Prayer, passages copied from the works of Jeremy Taylor, Lancelot Andrewes, and the *Eikon Basilike* (1649), recipes, anagrams, geographical and historical notes, and drawings. In addition to all this, interleaved or glued into the manuscript are a variety of printed sheets. Some of these, such as title pages, have been left whole; in other cases images and even lines of printed text have been cut and pasted into assemblages that are further embellished with manuscript annotations.

A single leaf provides a good example of Gibson's method (figure 8). At the top of fol. 190v he pasted two small emblems, one suggesting that time flees, the other that it turns with the year, with an explanatory text below: all three pieces have been cut from a single printed source and realigned on Gibson's page. In the middle of the page he pasted an illustration from John Booker's *Uranoscopia or an Almanack and Prognostication* (1649) that shows a roundel containing a man's body, labeled with twelve parts corresponding to the signs of the zodiac, and he then wrote on the whole composition, making manuscript additions in three places.

No one, not even Gibson himself, could fully describe the meanings on this page. Even if you could find, as Smyth could not, the source from which the printed emblems were cut, you would not be appreciably nearer to your goal, for there is already more here than could ever be accounted for. An emblem, which in this period usually comprises an image, a motto, and an explanatory verse, constructs its meaning not only through the tension and dialogue between the elements but also by playing in the gap between the familiar and the strange, by asking us to understand what is represented in terms of what is missing, and by requiring readers to adjudicate the relation between the detail and its context. Since the reading can no longer proceed in one direction, but must go back and forth in space and time, a full analysis of such a structure is interminable even before you begin to consider what is not being said, while the unspoken exerts decisive pressure on any occasion of its use. Here, for example, you might recognize the scythe and the serpent with its tail in its mouth as the insignia of Saturn, who reigned as a usurper on the condition that he left no living heir to prevent the throne from returning to its rightful line. A comfortable thought for an imprisoned Royalist like Gibson, but has he entertained it? If he is explicit elsewhere about his hopes for the restoration of the Stuart monarchy, here the sentiment is available but unexpressed, and seems to have arisen,

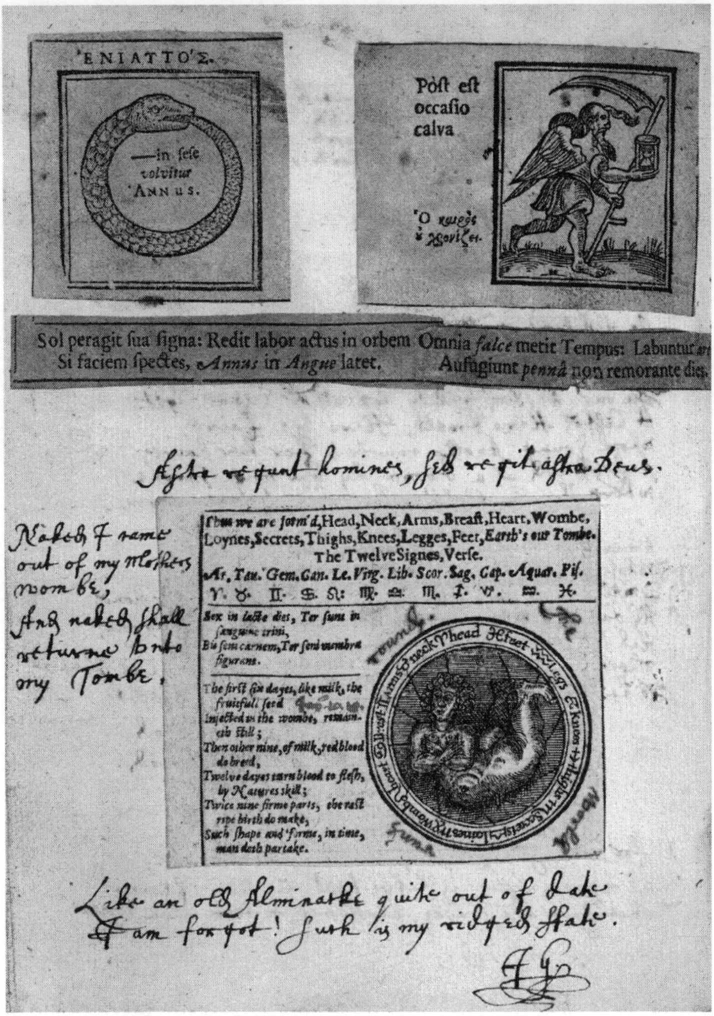

8. Folio page 19 v. from *The Commonplace book of Sir John Gibson*, composed in prison after 1655 of cut and pasted printed text with manuscript writing and signature in Gibson's hand.

on its own, from the circumstanced cut. "It's always a matter of encircling the absent word," says Derrida, talking about Genet, but also describing his own method of composition in *Glas*, and giving a good account of the potency of what is not said, of "letting it resound in the hollow of a bell, creating a void at the center of the space reserved for it, without ever writing, ever pronouncing what you are nevertheless constrained to understand, on one scene or the other, and what, consequently, strikes much more strongly, so as not to be mastered in the act" (*G* 128b–29b).

To cut and paste an emblem, as Gibson has done here, is to expand the horizons of its interpretative field in all directions, and to increase, at once the same time, both its reach and its local specificity. Where Booker's printed verse compares the child in utero to the burial of the soul in the body ("Earth's our tomb") Gibson's manuscript addition twists, elaborates, and personalizes the thought, stretching it, as it were, so that it becomes a place of consolation for one who had lost his worldly estates: "Naked I came out of my Mothers wombe, / And naked shall returne into my Tombe." Reacting to the signs of the zodiac, with its proposition that the actions of men are governed by ruling passions, he adds the thought that "the stars rule men, but God rules the stars"; and finally, drawing back from the almanac itself, whose cut pages, lying on the floor of his cell, must have been a poignant image of waste, he positions the whole as the emblem of his own situation: "Like an old Almanack, quite out of date, / I am forgot! such is my ridged [*sic*] fate."

All the sentiments that Gibson inscribes here are truisms, and conventionally formulated, but they are gathered into a dynamic whole, whose interactive parts repeatedly spark new meanings, while his signature, which lays claim to the page as a thing of his own making, marks it as a site where the personal is drawn out from the general. Historians of the book, who have recently learned to pay close attention to marginalia, might therefore judge the manuscript annotations to be the expression of Gibson's "true" or "original" thoughts, as opposed perhaps to the writing that had been taken from printed sources. But the poignant particularity that is achieved here is not an effect of Gibson's signature or of his manuscript annotations as marks of his presence. Rather, it rises from the depth and complexity of the cutting that he undertook and from the way in which the harvested details have been assembled into a scintillating formation whose movements no signature can close. That details that are treated this way "*enlarge*" or "desiglum" (unfold, gain potency, push against the borders of the cut that has produced them) as they are picked out and sewn into such a text is perhaps what is meant by the mysterious rhetorical trope of *energia*—the type of *detailing* that gives light and luster to an argument.[9]

All very well, but doesn't the cut destroy what it works on? It does; it must. Yet, even in relation to our archives, cutting has been a form of preservation since many of the textual fragments that survive for our scrutiny do so only because they were cut and repurposed. You might argue that preservation is not the right term, for cutting in even the most conservative of its modes is committed not to the retention of writing in its original state, but rather to its *renovation*. This, the question of what *remains* and how to keep it, returns us to Derrida, for it is not only the single theme of *Glas* but also the first point he makes in relation to what he calls archive fever.

Of this malady the earliest symptom is the realization that to preserve is to change—or, putting it more succinctly, that there is no preservation. Keep something in your possession and you have cut it off from the context that made it what it was; protect it from decay so that it survives its moment, hold it in its existing state, and (even or especially if you have kept it alive) you will find you have already wreaked violence upon it. Suppose, for example, that you want to conserve a violet. Certainly it can be done! You have only to consult a book such as Charles Estienne's *Maison Rustique*, published in Latin in 1564, in French in 1567, and translated into English in 1600 by Richard Surflet.

> You must take the fresh and new flowers of violets, and take from them their taile, and the little greene cup, by which they hang, and

> after drie them some small time in the shadow of the sunne, to take from them their superfluous moisture which they have: after that braie [grind] them in a stone mortar with twice so much sugar, and put them in a glasse vessel, which shall be set to sunne for the space of three moneths, and stirred very oft during the said time, as hath beene already said of the conserve of roses.

Perhaps this example, which suggests that what can be preserved can't be preserved, unless you want it as a conserve or jam, is excessive. "There is but seldome any preserves made of the flowers or leaves of herbes," notes Estienne, for the proper meaning of preserve is "the preserving of things whole and not stampt and beaten into one bodie."

Not flowers, then, nothing conserved as a jelly or paste: according to Estienne it is things like roots that can be properly preserved. The root of the Elicampane (*Inula Helenium*), for example:

> When you have taken up the roote in the moneth of October, at such time as it is very ripe, you must first take away all the sand and earth which is about it with a rough linen cloath, or with a strainer; after that you must scrape it al over with a very sharp knife, and according as the rootes are of bignes, to cleave them in two, three, more or less peeces of a fingers length, and boile them in a brasse cauldron with vinegar, and that in such sort as the slices may not burne within the cauldron. Three daies after they must be dried in the sunne, and put into a new pot well pitched, and cuted [*sic*] wine put unto them, and that so much, as they may be covered therwith, and a good deale of savourie pressed down upon them, and then the vessel close shut up and covered well with leather.[10]

The problem with preservation is that it destroys what it saves. However you do it, and whatever you call it, you cannot enjoy fresh local produce out of season.

This is no small point for literary critics, for it also describes our relation to the texts we read and those we want others to read. Did Derrida hope to be understood when he wrote *Glas?* Did he want others to understand what he was up to, or was the decision to write in double columns designed to secure his safety from being followed? Like Genet, whose writing career was interrupted when Sartre presumed to understand it, Derrida felt some antipathy to those who presumed to "get" him. But unlike Genet, perhaps, he wanted to be caught, "for if my text is (was) ungraspable, it will (would) be neither grasped nor retained" (*TP* 66). A text that was not somewhere retained—archived, preserved, read, *cut*—would be no text, it would be nothing at all. And Derrida would have been the first to understand that his own writings call for the curious form of survival that is their repurposing in projects such as my own.

So let's assume we have earned the right to say that cutting *preserves*. Immediately there are as many methods at our disposal as there are recipes in Estienne's comprehensive two-volume guide to country living. *Sign-sewing*—even before we consider the relation of arche-writing to the archive that it is we will have to tally up the forms of attachment at our disposal, all the ways in which we secure groups of letters and lines of writing, not only by linking them, writing them out, pasting, stitching, tucking, tying, bandaging, hiding them, storing them, or even sending them away, but also in less tangible ways, by seeing them, teaching them, pointing them out to others, memorizing, or otherwise knowing them. Furthermore, cutting and sewing must be thought together and with the proviso that one does not necessarily come before the other. "Take into account the overlap-effects [*effets de recoupe*]," says Derrida, where "*recoupe*" means cut again *and* reimburse or rebalance, "and you will see that the tissue ceaselessly reforms itself around the incision [*entaille*]" (*TP* 25). "*La couture et la recoupe*"—sewing and deducting—the seam cuts and the cut seams (*TP* 68b).

No sewing without cutting—this is the bitter logic of preservation as staged in the opening lines of *Glas* in relation to *remains*. What remains of Hegel's thought among those philosophers who cannot think (especially on the subject of remains) without him? What remains of Genet's text, once called "*what remained of a Rembrandt torn into small, very regular squares and rammed down the shithole*," which was largely destroyed by its author but whose remaining pages, published as a short piece in double columns, are now the focus of Derrida's split attention in his own double-columned *Glas* (*G* 1a, 1b)?

Derrida says there are two ways of dealing with remains. On the one hand you can assure, guard, assimilate, interiorize, idealize and "relieve" them. On the other, you can . . . leave them (*G* 1b–2b). "Keep them or throw them away," my mother would have said, "I don't care." And in fact, it is not clear that you have a choice, for either option runs the risk "of coming down to the same" (*G* 2b). All that wrapping and bolstering, all that sewing, all those preservatives and your effort at distillation, and you may find you have done nothing but intensify the problem. You have made the remains grow larger, and Derrida has a word for this, "*bander*," which means to have an erection, and also to bandage, swaddle, or wrap (*G* 23a). And there are certain situations, he notes, where "nothing comes about, where what surges up collapses 'at the same time,' where one can no longer cut through to a decision between the more and the less . . . Where one bands erect for nothing, where nothing bands erect, where the mere nothing 'bands erect'" (*G* 22b). Writing about Genet here, Derrida is also thinking, across the gutter that divides the columns of his text, about the Hegelian *Aufhebung*, the "airy ascent of the concept," "the retention of what slips away as it slips away," whereby matter is relieved, "raised, elevated, spiritualized, magnified, embalmed, interiorized, idealized, named" (*G* 23a, 10a, 8a). Mummified, in fact, according to a procedure that always seems comical to those who do not practice it, and can see it only as an absurd magnification and bloating of remains.

Actually, I think we will have to admit that cutting and sewing each have their comic sides, at least when viewed from the outside. Poking philosophical fun from one column to the other, *Glas* uses Hegel's discourse to expose the folly of Genet, and Genet's follies to expose Hegel's discourse, but neither comes out unscathed, or on top. And Derrida, the seamster, can himself no more leave an entity uncut than he can see a cutting without wanting to attach it, with loose stitches, into a new place. What is at play here, and what produces the scintillating effect of *Glas*, is not only that cutting and sewing are each both positive and negative, while neither of them can be simply set against philosophy (which has itself traditionally used the cut to delimit and dominate, while deploring the scissions of others)—it is that *there is something about tailoring that is always open to criticism*, that it is always on the edge of raising a laugh or an eyebrow. To me your cut looks reckless and your sewing overblown; you see that I have both cut and attached in the wrong place; and we both agree that our neighbor's patchwork is very much less than the sum of its parts.

The exemplary instance of *signacouture* is therefore *découpage*.[11] In sixteenth-century Venice the application of paper motifs to decorate walls, doors, and furniture in imitation of hand painting was a highly developed craft skill, but it is now better known as an amateur occupation that began to be popular among leisured women in the late seventeenth century. "We are here in the height of a new fashion," wrote a young French woman from Venice in 1710, "for cutting up colored engravings . . . every lady, great and small, is cutting away . . . we make wall-panels, screens and fireboards of them. There are books and engravings that cost up to 100 livres, and women are mad enough to cut up engravings worth 200 livres apiece. If this fashion continues, they will cut up Raphaels."[12] A decade later another letter writer advised his correspondents that the fashion in Paris is to want "nothing but decoupage . . . screens, folding screens, wall hangings, ceilings, the tops of coaches, and sedan chairs; it is being put everywhere. This fashion has made the prices of illustrations and prints rise to an extraordinary level."[13] You can see what will always be said to be wrong with it: as the hobby of foolish women découpage proceeds through the ignorant or callous ruination of original works, and even where this is clearly not the case découpage can still be said to drive up the price of prints, and so put them beyond the reach of those who would use them for proper and uncut purposes.

And the practice was not confined to France. In *A Supplement to the Queen-Like Closet* (1674), Hannah Woolley gives instructions on how to decorate the walls of a dining room. First, you must buy good black and white prints, "and cut them very exactly with a small pair of Cissors from the paper, [and] put them into a book as you do cut them." When you have prepared the surface of the wall, spread a thin layer of adhesive glaze on the back of your decals, and immediately "take them up with your knife, and so turn them into your hand, and clap them upon the Wainscot." "If you employ your fancy well," she adds, demonstrating the creative aspect of the art, you may make gardens, "fine stories," and imaginary landscapes, "or indeed anything you can imagine; for there is not any to be named, but you may find it in Prints, if you go to a shop that is well stored, nor no Pencil can shadow more rare than that will shew."[14] As the French examples suggest, smaller motifs were also cut and fixed onto pieces of furniture or other objects, and coated with several layers of varnish until the depth of the paper could no longer be seen or felt. Such work, which can be almost indistinguishable from wood inlay, requires significant expertise, but Woolley explains how something similar can be achieved at home. On walls, she advises, colored motifs "look Childishly, and too gay," but they are "good to put upon white Plates and Flower-pots for Closets" and to "dress up Glass-Plates":

> Take your Glass-Plates, and lay the right-sides downward upon a Table, then have in readiness some coloured Prints finely cut, and lay them on with Gum, with their right-sides to the wrong-side of the Plates; then take some Spanish-Whiting, mixed with Size which is purely cleer . . . then spread the same all over upon the Prints (not too thick) and when they are very dry, wipe the right side clean, and set them up in your Closet to use at your pleasure.[15]

Annealed under a shining surface, caught for attention like a fly in amber, its location rendered mysterious by the invisible substrate of varnish or glass, your motif appears, not like a paper flower stuck on a wall by a child, but as a special detail, marked and magnified by your attention, cited, assembled, *portentously glued*. (That this is an uncanny effect, sometimes disreputable, a display that hides a context but cannot help displaying the fact that the context has been hidden, is registered in Dickens's brief meditation on gentility in *Great Expectations* "no varnish can hide the grain of the wood, and the more varnish you put on, the more grain will express itself.")[16]

It is here that the relation of signacoupure and signacouture to literature can once more be grasped. But rather than these two terms, let's use the single term "sign-tailoring," for it will help us grasp cutting and stitching as a single, indissociable action. And then you can see what Derrida did not say, but what he has meant all along—that literature is sign-tailoring:

> The great stake of literary discourse—I do say discourse: the patient, crafty, quasi animal or vegetable, untiring, monumental, derisory too, but on the whole holding itself up to derision, transformation of the proper name, *rebus*, into things, into the name of things. The thing, here, would be the looking glass [*glace*], the ice [*glace*] in which the song sets, the heat of an appellation that bands itself erect [*se bande*] in the name. (*G* 5b)

Literature is a discourse that frames and stages the divisibility of the letter, while remarking the divisibility of its own framing—this is already enough to set it against the frames of philosophy. But this propensity to splinter its frame is not the only mark of literature's effect. Rather, it is in its capacity to enlarge the details of our obsessions (in its propensity to pick out and varnish figures from the general text) that we are most fully exposed to the example of literature's singular, risible, damaging, and restorative power.

4

Psychoanalytic Graphology

When Derrida argued that cultural graphology should accord "a certain privilege" to "researches of the psychoanalytic type," he was thinking in particular of those of Melanie Klein. "Klein's entire thematic, her analysis of the constitution of good and bad objects, her genealogy of morals could doubtless begin to illuminate, if followed prudently, the entire problem of the arche-trace, not in its essence (it does not have one), but in terms of valuation and devaluation" (*WD* 231). If you know a little bit about Klein (which may describe Derrida's own situation in the late 1960s), it is not hard to see where he thought this might go. For in her attention to a very early pregenital stage of development, when the child forms intense object relations to the world around it, Klein opened a new terrain between internal fantasy and external reality where psychoanalysis found itself circumstanced in a significantly more material and worldly environment than Freud had been able to envision for it. It is in this environment that Derrida always located the text, as indistinguishable from a universal structure of experience that he is here calling the *arche-trace*, and that we might describe as the structured experience of being altered.

In "The Violence of the Letter," in what is perhaps the most accessible passage in *Grammatology*, Derrida argues that writing appears "as soon as a society begins to live as a society, that is to say from the origin of life in general, when, at very heterogeneous levels of organization and complexity, it is possible to defer presence" (*Grammatology* 130–31). But what does it mean, to *defer presence?* Nothing more than to register and therefore archive information, in any actual or virtual place, or on any substance or surface. Presence is deferred, and the archive established, as life is lived—that is, in, on, or with any of the living and nonliving materials of the world as these interact with one another and with the nonmaterial (we might say "cultural") systems that are both their product and a new determinant of their future. Presence is always in the process of being altered and deferred by the archive that brings it into being, and this is what, from the beginning, Derrida meant by writing. It is not something added to or abstracted from experience, for the "privation of presence is the condition of experience, that is to say, of presence" (*Grammatology* 166).

But general as it is, this archiving alteration is always a local effect: it is the circumstanced condition of everything at every moment. And writing in the narrow sense is a strong form of *auto-affection* or *auto-immunity*, words Derrida often uses to describe the process whereby an individual organism alters and is altered by the worldly engagements that make it an outsider to its own inner life.[1] If Klein's work seemed important to Derrida in 1967 it was surely because, by describing the psychic investments that must hamper even the strictest ideal objectivity, it allows us to think about these circumstantial effects as they concern writing in the narrow sense. "To the extent that the constitution of ideal objectivity must essentially pass through the written signifier, no theory of this constitution has the right to neglect the investments of writing" (*Grammatology* 88). Here, in a residue of his first thesis, which was to have been called "The Ideality of the Literary Object," Derrida is thinking of Husserl's reading of Kant, where he argues that writing was not truth's additional and worldly *aide memoire* but a technique that ensures the ideality of meaning by liberating it from local contexts. What Derrida adds to their thought is the game-changing caution that writing's local investments cannot therefore be cast aside.[2] For they not only "retain a certain opacity in the ideality of the object" but are also the force that permits "the liberation of that ideality." It is the circumstanced temporality of writing, or what Derrida would elsewhere call the "determination of the trace" that gives "that force without which objectivity in general would not be possible" (*Grammatology* 88, translation modified). And these circumstances include, without being limited to, human affect: "In as much as it *puts into play* the presence of the present and the life of the living, the movement of language does not, one suspects, have only an analogical relationship with sexual auto-affection. It is entirely indistinguishable from it" (*Grammatology* 166–67).

Klein's work describes the mechanisms of projection and introjection that distort our apprehension and make us experience the things of the world as a return to our most primitive experience of parental figures, particularly the mother who sometimes gave and, as mothers must, sometimes withheld nurture, and so engendered feelings of love and gratitude, but also hatred and frustration, in her infant. Klein identified the body parts and other objects towards which the child's instincts are directed (often the breast or feces) and their most common substitutes (food, children, or money), arguing that as an infant perceives them, these "part-objects" are split into "good" and "bad" and fantastically endowed with powers of agency, so that they appear to persecute or comfort the self, other people, or even each other in response to the child's own feelings towards them.

Furthermore, Klein wrote about writing. In "Grammatology as a Positive Science," Derrida argued that cultural graphology could not proceed before it addressed some "preliminary" questions about writing as a material practice—for example, the question of the availability to an individual or group of diverse graphic forms and styles, the question of the relation of writing to diverse graphic substances and instruments, and the question of the place of writing within diverse institutional and social contexts (*Grammatology* 87–88). It may have been Marguerite Derrida who drew her husband's attention to Klein's description of the potent affective burden carried by these practices and institutions, but

Derrida was quick to see its potential: "As concerns the forms of signs, the cathexes of gestures, and of movements, of lines, points, and of the elements of the writing apparatus (instrument, substance, surface, etc.), a text like 'The Role of the School in the Libidinal Development of the Child' (1923) indicates the direction to be taken" (*WD* 231; *Grammatology* 88). The heightened and conflicting judgments heaped on writing over the centuries ("writing as sweet nourishment or as excrement, the trace as seed or mortal germ, wealth or weapon, detritus and/or penis, etc.") might be "illuminated," he suggested, if it were considered as a part object, tarred with an ambivalence derived from our very earliest feelings (*WD* 231).

Before we go to Klein's essay for help with these apparently "material" questions, let's note that the task is *already* theoretically challenging. It will not be enough to discover, as a bibliographer might, of what materials writing is made, or to point out, as a bibliographer might not, that writing can be baked and eaten, danced in the sand, or cut into fabric and skin. It will not even be enough to bear in mind what typographers have always known and what Roger Chartier and Donald McKenzie have more recently reminded historians of the book: that texts are interpreted by the way they are presented and transmitted, and that their "forms effect meaning."[3] For writing is an ideal object, which is to say that any local instance of it (say the occurrence of the letter "s") will only be itself (only be "s" and an instance of writing) if it can be repeated elsewhere—repeated in different fonts, hands, materials, and styles while still retaining, however minimally, the recognizable form of "s." Writing in the narrow sense is an action that is undertaken within the nested, institutional, and already given codes that allow it to appear, each time, as the relation of the singular instance to *what is already there and equally already gone*. So when Derrida suggested that Klein's "thematic" of object relations ("if followed prudently") might begin to illuminate the "entire problem of the arche-trace" this was not an invitation to think—in however complex or prudent a manner—simply about matter (*WD* 231).

Together with its companion piece "Early Analysis," "The Role of the School in the Libidinal Development of the Child" (1923) argues that even in normal children a wide range of scholastic actions and activities are subject to sexual cathexis and therefore to neurotic inhibitions. Athletic games of every sort "turned out to have a libidinal cathexis, and genital symbolism always played a part in it. The same applied of the road to school, the relation with men and women teachers, and also the relation to learning and teaching in themselves" (*LGR* 77). Klein observed that if children start failing at school or show a weakened inclination towards something they have previously enjoyed, it is not necessarily that they no longer like it, or now cannot understand it, but because they love something about it too well. The situation is not uncommon because a capacity for pleasure in any activity readily takes on a sexual-symbolic significance and so draws repression on itself. Once inhibition has set in, it spreads, both because a symbolic meaning is easily displaced onto new objects and activities and because as the child matures its extending ego-activities and interests acquire their own sexual-symbolic meanings and the scope for inhibition grows with them (*LGR* 73). All the same, without libidinal energy there would be no learning, no talent, no interests, and no meaningful activity of any kind (*LGR* 59). What determines whether a person develops a talent or, on the contrary, becomes inhibited and so disinclined to pursue it or to manifest neurotic or even psychotic symptoms in regard to it is their own capacity to sublimate superfluous libido—that is, to unfix libidinal fantasies from the particular objects, activities, and interests that have attracted them and transfer them to the their own ego-tendencies, where they can be given play and so discharged (*LGR* 86–88 passim).

As Klein (and after her Hannah Segal) went on to argue, sublimation is predicated on the development of symbolization from a destructively concrete form to one that can *represent an object without being equated with it*. Segal explained the difference using the example of two patients, one of whom says "he cannot play the violin because he will not masturbate in public," while the other can play even though it is clear that "to him, too, the violin represents the penis."[4] Like the man who cannot perform, Klein's young patients are stopped short by a symbolic equation between writing and some desired but prohibited aim. And a compendium of their inhibitions allows us to understand writing as a bodily product that appears outside the subject and seems to testify to its deepest impulses.

Derrida compiled such a list from Marguerite Derrida's translation of Klein's work and used it as a long footnote in *Grammatology* (333–34). For some children, writing was the equivalent of drawing libidinal actions and objects, while for others it permitted the unconscious creation of the objects or performance of the actions represented. And for some it was an expression of pleasure in movement. So when Fritz was writing, Klein observed, "the lines meant roads and the letters rode on motor-bicycles—on the pen—upon them. For instance, 'i' and 'e' ride together on a motor-bicycle that is usually driven by the 'i.'" Instead of the double "s" Fritz always wrote only one because, as Klein interpreted, the "one 's' was himself, the other his father. They were to embark together on a motor-boat, for the pen was also a boat, the copy-book a lake. The 's' that was himself got into the boat that belonged to the other 's' and sailed away in it quickly upon the lake" (*LGR* 63–65). Klein does not analyze the details of Fritz's driving fantasies, comment on the strange action whereby letters are simultaneously riding on the pen and deposited in place, or explain how "s" got away with the boat while remaining itself, but they suggest that for Fritz, as for others, writing not only gives rise to movement, and can picture movement, but that it can also awaken a movement response and thus be seen to move.

For the cultural graphologist, the consequence of Fritz's observation that a letter can be *both here and gone* is deeper and more general still, for it is an instance of what Derrida calls *iterability*—the fact that a sign is only itself to the extent that it can also function elsewhere, in different contexts. The boat is here, with me in it, and the boat is also elsewhere, perhaps sailing off so that I can look back at Daddy on the dock—or the game could be reversed, so that the letter, which is elsewhere, could be isolated from its instituted contexts and claimed as a particular thing, for example as the child's "own" small "s." (This, perhaps, is what Lacan meant by saying that the "materiality" of the letter was "peculiar," in that "we cannot say . . . that, like other objects, it must be or not be in a particular place but that unlike them it will be and not be where it is, wherever it goes" [*SPL* 55].)

In addition to the case histories Derrida cites, Klein discusses Felix, whose anxiety over masturbation was reflected in the fact that "he repeatedly omitted the concluding sentence" of his school exercise, "forgot something in the middle," or "compressed the whole lesson into the smallest possible compass"; Lisa, who had a taste for mathematics but was baffled by addition, for she could grasp "that one joins with another when both were the same" but could not see how they were to be added up when they were different; and Fritz (in reality Klein's own son Erich), who had a marked inhibition in doing division sums (he knew perfectly well how to do them, yet always got them wrong). No wonder:

> He told me once that in doing division he had first of all to bring down the figure that was required and he climbed up, seized it by the arm and pulled it down. To my inquiry as to what it said to that he replied that quite certainly it was not pleasant for the number—it was as if his mother stood on a stone 13 yards high and someone came and caught her by the arm so that they tore it out and divided her.

Fritz confided that "actually every child wants to have a bit of his mother," who is distributed to be eaten among her children, and Klein interpreted for him that he confused the remainder of this feast "with the quotient in division, and always wrote it in the wrong place, because in his mind it was bleeding pieces of flesh with which he was unconsciously dealing." Lisa would have understood: "it had always seemed so difficult to her to divide a quite big number by a smaller but also big one, and it was particularly hard if there was an incomplete remainder. She associated to this a horse, a horrible animal with a hanging mutilated tongue, cropped ears, etc., that wanted to jump over a fence, an idea that aroused her own most violent resistances" (*LGR* 64, 67, 69–70).

In her analyses of these cases Klein notes that, beyond or before the genital significance of the instruments of writing, other component instincts such as "peeping" in reading or aggressive sadistic tendencies in writing also come into play (*LGR* 66–67). In fact, any given instance of reading or writing involves a congeries of primitive instinctual drives as these originate in different organic sources and undergo the vicissitudes that allow them to alight on various objects or gain expression through various actions within various institutions. And finally, the drives have local histories, for while the object of an instinctual aim is very variable and relatively interchangeable, it may become highly particularized during the life of a person as the only thing that will procure satisfaction. A baby—any baby—will satisfy a variety of instinctual aims, and a dog may do almost as well, but once that dog or baby has become specific to its parents, *only* it will do, even as it continues to be endowed with new meanings in accordance with the process Freud called deferred action. Each instinctual expression has its singular moment in a local history, and taking these tenets together we might say that there are as many instinctual expressions as there are individual actions all told. (Here we could marvel again at the poverty of the metaphors we use to describe writing—what are you doing with that pen, Mommy? Just weaving, darling!)

It should be clear by now that "object relations," the type of psychoanalysis pioneered by Klein, is a not a theory of objects but a theory of feelings and affects. D. W. Winnicott clarified the argument of his famous essay "Transitional Objects and Transitional Phenomena" (1953) by pointing out that it is not the object that is transitional but *the child* who uses the transitional object, its first "not-me" possession, to explore the area of experience between its internal feelings and the world outside. He proposed that the relation between inner thoughts and external reality, such as might be perceived by two people in common, is never fully resolved, so that transitional phenomena persist into later life, where playing, artistic activities, religious feelings, dreaming, drug addiction, and a variety of obsessional rituals allow individuals the respite of an unchallenged "intermediate area of experience," in which the question of the difference between inner and outer realities is suspended.[5] At the risk of obscuring what is specific about the transitional phenomena, this list might be broadened. For any use of technology and any interaction with the environment could be experienced as such an "intermediate area."

Writing in all its forms is a strong case of the experience of not having to decide, or even ask ourselves, if we are dealing with subjective or objective reality. Indeed, the fact that it works to produce and sustain an "intermediate environment" is surely a consequential determinant in the relation of writing to literature as a protected state of irresponsibility—one in which, as Derrida and others have argued, the writer is (if only in principle) licensed to say "everything he wants or everything he can" (*SI* 37). Before there can be any question of responsibility, writing protects readers and writers from their own knowledge of what is, and what is not, part of the external world, and it is because any text can do this for anyone that we will never be able to adjudicate what is, and what is not, a work of literature. Furthermore, it is because the forms of writing are there *before we use them and only because we use them* that they accrue their strangely potent status as objects in our world. We love and hate words as our own and hate and love them because they are not our own, and we miss them even as we have them.

In his footnote to Klein, Derrida also pointed to James Strachey's essay "Some Unconscious Factors in Reading" (1930), which follows Klein in an attempt to isolate the "special determinants" that produce inhibitions in reading in "even approximately normal people." Strachey describes a patient who read with a pencil in hand, ticking off each page as he finished, then read again and confirmed the second reading by putting a cross through the tick ("This was when he was in a particularly good state. . . . If things were going badly or if he was reading something especially important every word had to have its tick."). Another patient, a professional proofreader, was "perpetually haunted by the feeling of having missed some misprint of a disastrous sort, and was thus obliged to go through the galleys over and over again."[6] Strachey's entertaining piece was presented to the British Psycho-Analytical Society in 1930, where it must have provoked laughter as well as discussion, but its serious point drew on Klein's recent attention to the destructive as well as to the more simply libidinal impulses that characterize a child's thought. For Strachey proposed that reading, which "is a way of eating another person's words," corresponds to two stages of the infant's oral phase, "a pre-ambivalent one where everything seems to go smoothly, and an ambivalent one where difficulties arise at every step." If, in this second phase, sublimation is unstable or incomplete, "there will be an immediate tendency to the release of a number of sadistic and destructive impulses." Each word will be felt to be "an enemy that is being bitten up" and so become threatening and dangerous in its turn, even as the reader is simultaneously "loving" words, "rolling them round in his mouth and eventually making them part of himself."[7]

Klein quickly endorsed this argument, and enlarged its reach:

> J. Strachey has shown that reading has the unconscious significance of taking knowledge out of the mother's body, and that the fear of robbing her is an important factor for inhibition in reading. I should like to add that it is essential for a favorable development of the desire for knowledge that the mother's body should be felt to be well and unharmed. It represents in the unconscious the treasure-house of everything desirable which can only be got from there; therefore if it is not destroyed, not so much in danger and therefore not so dangerous itself, the wish to take food for the mind from it can be more easily carried out. (*LGR* 241)

And here, in the aftermath of the vicissitudes of love and aggression, incorporation or projection, eating and voiding, a new possibility emerges: the release of knowing that something other than the self is out there, more or less intact in spite of the predations of our own demands. Beyond the infant's panic at the loss of the other, and beyond our own mature but myopic directives to consider or contact that other (directives that are themselves caught up in the dance of object relations), we might discern the outline of a different ethical proposition—namely, that the preservation of what we feel to be good is determined less by ourselves than by its own capacity for survival.

Winnicott, whose work and presence exercised a powerful influence over both André Green and Marguerite Derrida's training analyst Joyce McDougall, was developing something like this thought in the years immediately before Derrida presented "Freud and the Scene of Writing" to Green's seminar.[8] Winnicott was concerned with what he called the "environment mother," a maternal function that can be distinguished from the "object mother" (the "object or owner of the part-object that may satisfy the child's urgent needs") by its consistent provision of stability. The environment mother "wards off the unpredictable and . . . provides care in handling and general management"; she facilitates her child's growth through the reliability of her presence; and she allows her child the crucial experience of "being alone while someone else is present."[9] In his important essay, "The Capacity to be Alone," Winnicott argued that the state of being alone was not a fear to be overcome or a wish to be indulged but a capacity that is "nearly synonymous with emotional maturity"—it is the ability to feel alone but not forsaken. The provision of an environment that allows this experience, for example as the gift of a loving and present therapeutic nonintervention, came to assume an increasingly important place in Winnicott's thought and practice, and it was further theorized by Wilfred Bion, who used Keats's term "negative capability" to describe the therapist's capacity to listen without rushing to interpret and a healthy person's ability to remain intact in the face of not knowing while thinking.[10]

Could we conclude that any text that functions as an environment mother is a work of literature? It is at least clear that a literary text *can* function in this way. But it is also remarkable how clearly Derrida's own writing is built on, and requires of its readers, the same combination of close attention and suspended knowledge that characterized the clinical practice of Winnicott and other members of the British School of Psychoanalysis. I always begin teaching Derrida by promising students that, if they put in the effort, they will know less by the end of the semester, and be wiser by knowing less. That there is something in every thought that is not given us to know, and that this is cause for rejoicing rather than panic or stoic resignation, is a position Derrida maintained until the end of his career. Properly understood, it is a cure for archive fever, an antidote to the irruptions of Derrida's own anxieties about the passing of time, and a thought that cultural graphologists might use, one day, to develop a minimum impact theory of reading and writing.

It is hard to imagine that outside Klein's own case histories you could find her narrative of love, hostility, and guilt more vividly registered than in the flower-conscious work of John Conway. As the full title of the first edition explains, it contains "*Meditations and praiers, gathered out of the sacred letters, and virtuous writers: disposed in the fourme of the alphabet of the queene majesties name. Whereunto are added comfortable consolations.*"[11] A work of acrostics, a set of prayers and self-counsel, a commonplace book, an autobiography, a lament from prison, a self-justification, a bid for attention, and a warning to others, the work is the medium through which its author expresses his sense of having been misjudged and his feelings of abandonment. His guilt has nothing to do with the cause of his incarceration, about which he continues to protest his innocence in terms that suggest the primal fantasies by which he is driven: "to the very case of my committing, wherein I am wounded, maymed, wronged and lost . . . I professe before the Almighty as innocent as the Childe inseparate his Mothers intrayles." The responsibility Conway does accept concerns the fact that his "unclean and unfaithful soul" forsook the "living water" of God's love to dig for itself "muddy pits," and he repeatedly begs his Heavenly Father to forget "the contempt and injury," and take him back into His "bosome of bounty and loving kindnesse." Such sentiments, and the tropes through which they are expressed, are conventional, but one can never be sorry enough, and Conway's skill as a writer allows him to fill prayer after prayer without exhausting his passion.

The fact that many of these prayers are acrostics on the Queen's name underlines their strangely doubled address, whereby they seem to be directed as much to Elizabeth as to God: "Deliver me from false surmises, and accusations of me: rule me after thine own will and pleasure," "I cast not Petitions before thee, hoping in mine own Merites, but trusting in thy great mercies and sweet promises," "I am not able to abide thy heavy displeasure, if thou chastise me with thy Rodde of justice I perish." Although Conway's biography is unreliable, and the circumstances of his incarceration unknown, an Elizabethan prisoner faced the real likelihood of death in appalling conditions unless he could procure the Queen's mercy.[12] But Conway's feelings about this reality are expressed using metaphors of dirt and sweetness, injury and nourishment that are redolent of primitive anxieties. He accounts for himself as if he were a small child fearing retribution from both parents, although slightly less frightened of his father, to whom he is still able to talk: "To this day, from my birthe, thow knowest, Lorde, I have served her with true hart and innocent handes." The prayers typically address the injured mother (who perhaps won't listen) inside the father (who might), and we don't need to be early-modern Protestants, Elizabethan subjects, or believers of any sort to understand their position:

> I am unworthy to be called thy Creature, or one whom the Earthe should susteine, or nourishments yeelde their naturall foode. Marveile it is (oh Lorde) that thy Creatures and Elementes, do not revenge the iniurie, and contempte which I have made thee, through my manifolde iniquitie. But nowe, moste loving Father, have mercy (I beseeche thee) . . . Open to me thy besome of bounty and lovinge kindnesse, and replenish me with the nourishment and solace of thy grace.

To have read Klein is to understand why Conway's anxieties still resonate with us: it is because we have all been there.

According to Klein the sadistic fantasies directed against the inside of the mother's body constitute the child's "first and basic relation to the outside world," while a mature adaptation to reality depends "upon the degree of success" with which the subject entertains and then passes through this phase of love, guilt, and anxiety (*LGR* 221). How is this adaptation achieved? Klein proposed that side by side with the destructive impulses there exists "a profound urge to make sacrifices, in order to help and to put right loved people who in fantasy have been harmed or destroyed." Although such reparation is a largely imaginary activity, it has real effects in the world, for it involves dealing with the sufferings of the past by doing to others what you wish had been done to you. Our grievances against the parents who frustrated our wishes, the feelings of hate to which these gave rise, and the guilt we then felt for wanting to injure the parents we loved, "all these . . . we may undo in retrospect . . . by playing at the same time the parts of loving parents and loving children." Meanwhile, "in our unconscious phantasy we make good the injuries we did in fantasy, and for which we may unconsciously still feel very guilty." Klein regarded this combined process of imaginary and practical action, which she called making reparation, to be a fundamental element in every positive human relationship (*LGR* 312–13).

But the ways to repair are many, and not all of them require the presence of another human, especially in Klein's scheme, where "things represent human beings, and therefore are things of anxiety" (*LGR* 213). Anyone who can symbolize can make reparation. Klein's patients used drawing and painting "as means to make people anew," and she elaborated the point using the story of Ruth Weber, whose career as an artist began when she painted a portrait of Josephine Baker in the space left on her walls when her brother-in-law retrieved a painting he had lent her. The gap had seemed "to coincide with the empty space within" that had haunted Weber for her whole life, while her experience of filling it produced an "unspeakable sense of happiness." While it is the *content* of this and the subsequent paintings by Weber that best alerts us to their reparative motive (for they are mostly portraits of women, including her own mother), for Klein it is the action of painting that in this case repairs the rents "in the fabric of the world" that the anxious child feared she had inflicted (*LGR* 93, 215–17).

That writing can be reparative goes without saying, but that one of its modes of reparation is to fill space is worth underlining.

The conditions under which Conway wrote must have made him particularly conscious of this task and its therapeutic benefits, for having been deprived of writing materials in prison he was forced to compose his prayers in soft pencil on his wooden trencher. He must either have memorized each section as it was finished, or passed it to a visitor to be copied, and then wiped out the draft to make room for the next, for he tells his readers that, lacking all other means "to bring to thy gratefull hande this small quantitie of Spirituall foode," he often had to take his meals "without use of any Trencher." As a prisoner Conway could not take writing materials for granted; he had first to devise a receptive surface to sustain and contain the marks left by his pencil, and then find a way of smuggling his compositions into the world beyond. You could imagine that he came to love the trencher board that supported and controlled his efforts, exerting constraint by resisting and absorbing the marks of his soft pencil, limiting the size of the textual units he could compose, and forcing him to accept the penance of eating from his hands so that the space could be reserved for writing. Like an ideal listener, or like Winnicott's environment mother, the trencher would have received and regulated Conway's protestations of innocence and grief, stopping him when he had said enough, withholding its own interpretations, remaining undamaged as it first contained and then, when he was ready, let his prayers go. Few living companions could have done as much—perhaps, in his freedom, he missed his wooden friend.

It may even have been in an effort to reproduce the security of a straitened and therefore fillable space that Conway, or his printer for him, set his book within a skeleton frame of type ornament (in such a composition the frame is retained and re-used for each sheet, and the lines of text are set within and according to the limits it imposes). Such settings are common enough for English prayer books in the period, and Conway might have envisioned or requested that his own text be set in such a manner. Certainly he was concerned with the typographical space in which it was assembled. In a curious letter to the reader he regrets having been forced by press of business to leave the work unfinished. As a result, he has had to "estrange" from the Queen "the finall partes of this small peece," and must now offer the reader additional material "in supplie of," (that is, in the place of) "void paper." Void paper? The work is by no means short or noticeably truncated, and had he not raised it you would not have found anything missing. Conway asks us to accept the "few selected sentences" from Scripture and other ancient sources that comprise the addition because they are worthy enough in themselves, may be of use to the reader, and are "lesse labor" to him. At least, he hopes, undoing these justifications, they will be "better placed than barraine paper." But why must the blank paper be there? Perhaps the printer wanted to set additional words so that he did not smudge the final pages or waste part of the last sheet printed.

Whatever the reason for the new material, Conway knows it is a stopgap, and feels its inadequacy. He suggests its sentences should be first skimmed, then read with a judicious eye, "to read, and unreade them, to imbrace the good and eschewe the ill." This is a conventional method for dealing with pagan sources, and particularly appropriate in a volume that mixes scriptural and secular writing, but it also suggests Conway's ambivalence about the way he has tried to fill up the text, using words that may not do what he needs them to do, and could be dispensed with if he had anything better. Reparation or stumbling block, an island of security or a drop into the void—a word can be any of these things, and it's not easy to tell which one it is going to be until it has produced its effects. Who knows what a word is, of what size or density, how far it can be stretched, what void it can fill? Who knows what lies beneath its surface, except in the very moment that they put their own weight on it? We all write by composing words in spaces, and Conway's struggle to close and secure his text suggests how radically precarious such assemblages can be.

How is writing secured? There is much to be considered about the forces and technologies that bind it. But before we could address these problems another must be opened: when it comes to writing, *where and what is it on?*

When historians of the book think rigorously about writing they quickly arrive at the thought that there is no writing except against a background. Stone, wax, clay, skin, plaster, paper . . . the background could also be air in which we see smoke particles, darkness as contrasted with light, or water that briefly holds and marks the passage of colored ink. We might go so far as to say that the relation of writing to its support is even present when it is a question of ink in ink, or water in water, a drop in the ocean, although at this point you can see that the concept of "support" is too local, too parochial, too un-thought to *sustain* (there it is again) everything that we might want to understand about writing and its backgrounds. Certainly bibliographers might give the matter more thought, for as Derrida remarks in a footnote to his late essay "Paper or Me," *biblion* originally meant not "book" or "work" but a support for writing: "in Greek, *biblos* is the internal bark of the papyrus, just as in Latin *liber* originally designated the living part of the bark" (*PM* 187).

Let's focus on this remark. What "biblos" and "liber" designate is not bark as in rind but the interior pith or vascular tissue of the plant that provides the fibrous matter for papermaking. "Biblos" is the Greek name for the spongy wetland sedge from which papyrus was prepared, first by discarding the tough outer layer of the stalk, and then by slicing the soft inner core into broad, thin strips, which were pressed, soaked, and woven into sheets—no glue necessary, since the sugars in the papyrus bond the strips into a sheet that, once it has been pressed for a few days, is so pale, smooth and flexible that you can easily see how it earned its name in hieroglyphics: "baby skin." To understand this process is to appreciate the conceptual crux at which Derrida hints when he describes biblos as coming from the "internal bark" of the papyrus. For in that brief, oxymoronic phrase, the pith of the plant—that is, the life-sustaining network of channels and responsive cells through which the sap rises—is exposed and externalized. Which means that you never see biblos alive; as it rises from the depths it dies. Its soft core flayed and hardened as it is prepared to receive writing, the infantine suppleness of papyrus is rediscovered only on the far side of its death.

So here's a thought to entertain as we continue to juggle with the metaphors that are all we know or will know about writing: if biblos is dead *before* it is subjected to the marks of the pen, perhaps it is not, after all, the letter that kills but contact with the dead surface that kills *it*. Why does the hand pause before it marks a new sheet? If our conscious motive is to protect the pristine writing surface from the uses that destroy it, our unconscious thought is that if we hurt or impair that surface, it may seek to destroy us. But beyond such fears lies perhaps another—that biblos, far from being angry and seeking revenge, is entirely and permanently indifferent to our efforts. And here you can see that it is not going to be so easy to distinguish Winnicott's environment mother from the "object mother," for a mother who fails to provide the environment where the child can grow to be himself is a *bad environment mother*, and so an "object mother." Hard, repellent, dead before we get there, biblos does not care, it does not even know, that we might consider ourselves to be in relation with it. Perhaps this is what drains life from letters, so that they shrivel and drop, unattended, from surfaces that refuse to sustain them.

As a machined contrivance of different surfaces, and the passage through impression between them, printed writing has always provoked the question of the substrate and carried the burden of anxiety that can attach to it. Look closely at a book that has been printed on a letter press and you will see that the black lines of the letters have been punched into the surface of the paper when it was pressed down onto the type, and now lie slightly behind it. The page is in three dimensions, and the result is visually consequential, as Robert Bringhurst explains: "the color and sheen of the ink join with the smooth texture of the crushed paper, recessed into the white and rougher fibres surrounding the letters . . . The black light of the text *shines out* from within a well-printed letterpress page."[13] Even where it is merely *laid on* paper (a strange arrangement, when you think about it), writing is the picture of a paradoxical space—a surface without volume that is riddled with holes and raised into peaks and valleys by the contours of the line.

In his own preface to *Un coup de dés* Mallarmé described what he saw as the consequence of leaving so much paper blank in the layout of his poems: "the literary value, if I am allowed to say so, of this print-less distance which mentally separates groups of words or words themselves, is to periodically accelerate or slow down the movement, the scansion, the sequence."[14] Derrida followed Mallarmé and other critics in admiring each page as if it were the portrait of a desert vista, sparsely sown with oases of words, the white spaces causing a temporal pause that has to be crossed on the way to the next word (M 115). But we don't have to accept this reading of the space. "White wall/black hole? . . . depending on the combinations, the wall could just as well be black, and the hole white," note Deleuze and Guattari in the course of their meditation on the process of "subjectification."[15] What if we reverse the visual polarity of Mallarmé's pages? The white, that had been nothing but ground for the figures of the words, would spring to the front as a strange lace punched with holes. And now what is "blank" is not the space *between* words but the inked words themselves, and these are no longer surface shapes but something more dizzying: black holes that open onto shafts, stratified histories, vertical axes down which meaning is attracted and disappears. Here it is not words that are assembled in space but space that is assembled inside words. Words are burrows, tunnels, funnels, passages, expanding territories, and folding stars. It is a wonder that any of us can read.

A strange thing, the page, but we have not needed Derrida or Mallarmé to tell us this. *Tristram Shandy*, a book whose comic effect depends in part on its determination to hinder our reading of it, is celebrated for containing, among other "experimental" effects, a completely black leaf. This has been described by one modern critic as a "startling gesture of absolute opacity," but since it follows a description of the tombstone of Parson Yorick, who died slandered and broken-hearted, it can also be read as a figure for the inexpressibility of Tristram's grief, for the overflowing of his feelings, or even for the ink that was used to traduce and overwhelm his friend. Ascribing meanings like this to the black page we do as advised by Tristram, who tells us that "many opinions, transactions and truths" lie "mysteriously hid" under its "dark veil." But he is an unreliable narrator and has here laid a trap for the unwary, for the page is only a conventional mourning leaf, such as was commonly used by printers to accompany printed elegies, funeral sermons, or other records of death. To follow Tristram's advice and speculate on what the black page means is thus to be caught searching for "transactions and truths" in an object whose message is only too clear.

Nevertheless, if Tristram is joking, Sterne is not. For when it is relocated within the pages of a novel, the black leaf stages the entire mystery of the page itself, not only as a support for our intellectual and affective projections but as an object whose ubiquity prevents us from noticing its oddity. The earliest black page to survive in England is that which comprises the front cover of Thomas Middelton's satire of London life, *The Blacke Booke* (London, Thomas Creede for Jeffrey Chorlton, 1604) (figure 9).[16] It is already in a playful mood, designed to "re-mark" the dark deeds of the Londoners: "I call this the Black Booke," says Middleton, "because it doubly damns the divel" by showing that the citizens are worse than the denizens of Hell.[17] In a final address the book itself asks the reader "am I blacke ynough, thinke you, drest up in a lasting suite of Incke? Do I deserve my Darke and pitchy Tytle?"[18] The title, date, border, and ornament of the title page to which our attention is thus drawn have been produced by intaglio cutting, a process of wood cutting that reverses normal procedures. To prepare a normal woodcut, the background of the image must be cut away, leaving raised the lines to be inked; in intaglio or white-line cutting the lines are incised below the surface of the woodblock, and perhaps protected with wax or oil against picking up ink. What then appears as writing, white letters on a black ground, is the absence of ink, which gives us the impression of looking through the page, as if to a second surface underneath. The effect, which was sometimes exploited by printers when they were printing memorial material, is an uncanny or ghostly one, and it teaches us to see writing as the interruption of a surface, an

9. Black title page with white title and imprint date produced by intaglio cutting for Thomas Middleton. *The Blacke Booke* (London: Thomas Creede for Jeffrey Chorlton, 1604).

affair of pinking, slashing, or cutting away material—a découpage of the uncut page (figure 10).

Although it has not survived in any of the copies still extant, *The Blacke Booke* was also furnished with a black end page. We rarely remember that early modern printed books were sold with paper or cardboard covers to protect and advertise their contents. Some were in the form of binders' wrappers, which could be used on any book of the same size; some were publishers' wrappers, which were designed to wrap works from a single printer; others

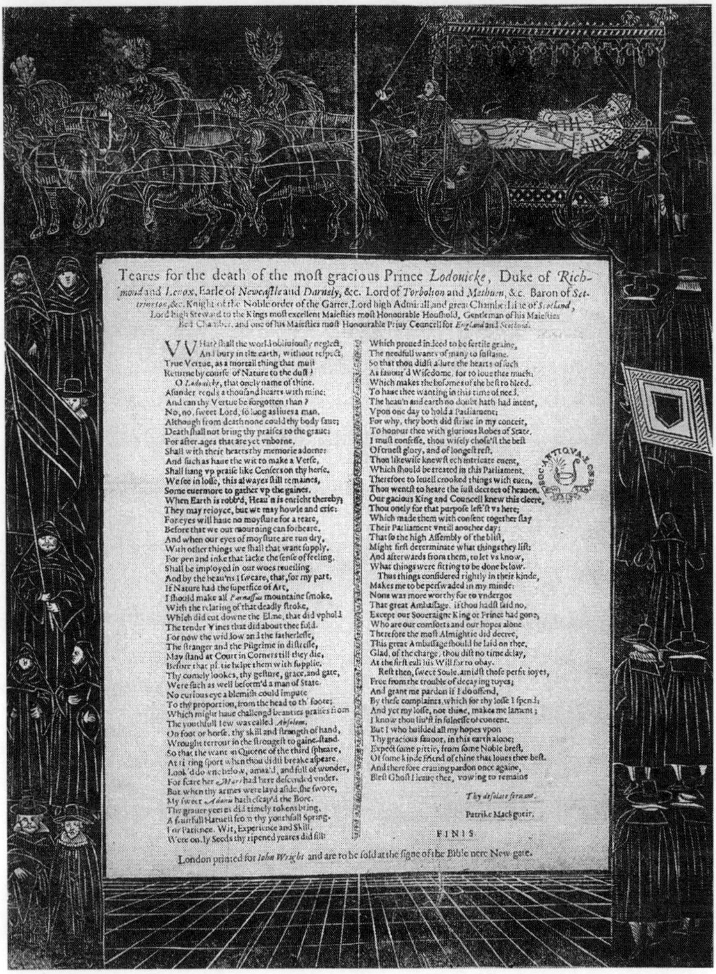

Teares for the death of the most gracious Prince *Lodouicke*, Duke of *Richmond* and *Lenox*, Earle of *Newcastle* and *Darnely*, &c. Lord of *Torbolton* and *Methuen*, &c. Baron of *Settrinton*, &c. Knight of the Noble order of the Garter, Lord high Admirall, and great Chamberlaine of *Scotland*, Lord high Steward to the Kings most excellent Maiesties most Honourable Houshold, Gentleman of his Maiesties Bed Chamber, and one of his Maiesties most Honourable Priuy Councell for *England* and *Scotland*.

VVHat? shall the world obliuiously neglect,
And bury in the earth, without respect,
True Vertue, as a mortall thing that must
Returne by course of Nature to the dust?
O *Lodouicke*, that onely name of thine.
Asunder rends a thousand hearts with mine:
And can thy Vertue be forgotten than?
No, no, sweet Lord, so long as liues a man.
Although from death none could thy body saue;
Death shall not bring thy praises to the graue:
For after-ages that are yet vnborne,
Shall with their hearts thy memorie adorne:
And such as haue the wit to make a Verse,
Shall hang vp praise like Censers on thy herse.
We see in losse, this alwayes still remaines,
Some euermore to gather vp the gaines.
When Earth is robb'd, Heau'n is enricht thereby;
They may reioyce, but we may howle and crie:
For eyes will haue no moysture for a teare,
Before that we our mourning can forbeare.
And when our eyes of moysture are run dry,
With other things we shall that want supply.
For pen and inke that lacke the sense of feeling,
Shall be imployed in our woes reuelling
And by the heau'ns I sweare, that, for my part,
If Nature had the superfice of Art,
I should make all *Parnassus* mountaine smoke,
With the relating of that deadly stroke,
Which did cut downe the Elme, that did vphold
The tender Vines that did about thee fold.
For now the widdow and the fatherlesse,
The stranger and the Pilgrime in distresse,
May stand at Court in Corners till they die,
Before that pitie helpe them with supplie.
Thy comely lookes, thy gesture, grace, and gate,
Were such as well beseem'd a man of State.
No curious eye a blemish could impute
To thy proportion, from the head to th' foote;
Which might haue challeng'd beauties praises from
The youthfull Iew was called *Absolom*.
On foot or horse, thy skill and strength of hand,
Wrought terrour in the strongest to gaine-stand.
So that the wanton Queene of the third spheare,
At tilting sport when thou didst breake a speare,
Look'd downe below, amaz'd, and full of wonder,
For feare her *Mars* had here descended vnder.
But when thy armes were layd aside, she swore,
My sweet *Adonis* hath escap'd the Bore.
Thy grauer yeeres did timely tokens bring,
A fruitfull Haruest from thy youthfull Spring.
For Patience, Wit, Experience and Skill,
Were onely Seeds thy ripened yeares did fill:
Which proued indeed to be fertile graine,
The needfull wants of many to sustaine.
So that thou didst allure the hearts of such
As fauour'd Wisedome, for to loue thee much:
Which makes the bosomes of the best to bleed,
To haue thee wanting in this time of need.
The heau'n and earth no doubt hath had intent,
Vpon one day to hold a Parliament:
For why, they both did striue in my conceit,
To honour thee with glorious Robes of State.
I must confesse, thou wisely chose'st the best
Of truest glory, and of longest rest.
Thou likewise knewst ech intricate euent,
Which should be treated in this Parliament,
Therefore to leuell crooked things with euen,
Thou wentst to heare the iust decrees of heauen.
Our gacious King and Councell knew this cleere,
Thou onely for that purpose left'st vs here;
Which made them with consent together stay
Their Parliament vntill another day:
That so the high Assembly of the blist,
Might first determinate what things they list:
And afterwards from them, to let vs know,
What things were fitting to be done below.
Thus things considered rightly in their kinde,
Makes me to be perswaded in my minde:
None was more worthy for to vndergoe
That great Ambassage, if thou hadst said no,
Except our Soueraigne King or Prince had gone,
Who are our comforts and our hopes alone
Therefore the most Almightie did decree,
This great Ambassage should be laid on thee,
Glad, of the charge, thou didst no time delay,
At the first call his Will for to obay.
Rest then, sweet Soule, amidst those perfit ioyes,
Free from the trouble of decaying toyes;
And grant me pardon if I do offend,
By these complaints, which for thy losse I spend;
And yet my losse, not thine, makes me lament;
I know thou liu'st in fulnesse of content.
But I who builded all my hopes vpon
Thy gracious fauour, in this earth alone;
Expect some pittie, from some Noble brest,
Or some kinde friend of thine that loues thee best.
And therefore crauing pardon once againe,
Blest Ghost I leaue thee, vowing to remaine

Thy desolate seruant,

Patrike Mackgueir,

FINIS

London printed for *Iohn Wright* and are to be sold at the signe of the Bible nere New-gate.

10. Patrick Mackguear, *Teares for the death of the most gracious Prince Lodovick, Duke of Richmond and Lenox, Earle of Newcastle and Darnly, etc.* (London: for John Wright, 1624). Broadsheet with intaglio wood cut showing the funeral procession of the Duke of Richmond.

are now called integrated wrappers, for they were printed with the work, on the recto of the first leaf of the first quire and the verso of the last leaf of the last quire, so that when the book was folded and assembled these pages appeared as its outer wrappers.[19] Such covers were temporary, and usually discarded when the work was given a more permanent binding, but among those that survive are a significant number of mourning wrappers. The earliest I have found are in two copies of Samuel Daniel's *A Funerall poem Upon the death of the late noble Earle of Devonshire* (London: s. n., 1606), where the poem is preceded by a black title page with white intaglio border and writing; the Huntington copy retains its final leaf that is black on the verso, which completes the wrapper.[20] But the production of mourning wrappers may have begun earlier. The British Library copy of Henry Petow's elegy for Queen Elizabeth, *Êlizabeth quasi vivens: Eliza's funeral* (London: E. Alde for M. Lowe, 1603) has heavy ink smudging on its first and last pages, which suggest lost mourning wrappers; while the death of the Prince of Wales in 1612 elicited a spate of black titles sufficient to suggest that the practice was in full fashion by then. Used to accompany mourning texts, black pages like this would have made an appropriate (and not inexpensive) show of grief: poems and sermons so dressed might be pinned to the coffin or hearse, or handed out to the mourners at a funeral.

Several of the elegies for Henry also include *internal* leaves that have been bisked in ink (that is, printed from the uncut back of a woodcut block) on one or both sides, to make black pages. Such pages could operate inside books as moveable partitions. Their location within mourning volumes was not always set, and they now survive bound at different places in different copies of the same work, carrying a powerful force of affect at a place where words fail. For example, the black verso pages that punctuate Sylvester's *Lachrymae Lachrymarum* (1612) or Tourneur's "Griefe on the Death of Prince Henry" (1612) produce a series of openings, a rhythm where the little that can be said is interspersed with a set of silences or absences that seem to acknowledge, as John Taylor puts it in his own black-paged elegy for the Prince, "Alas, alas,

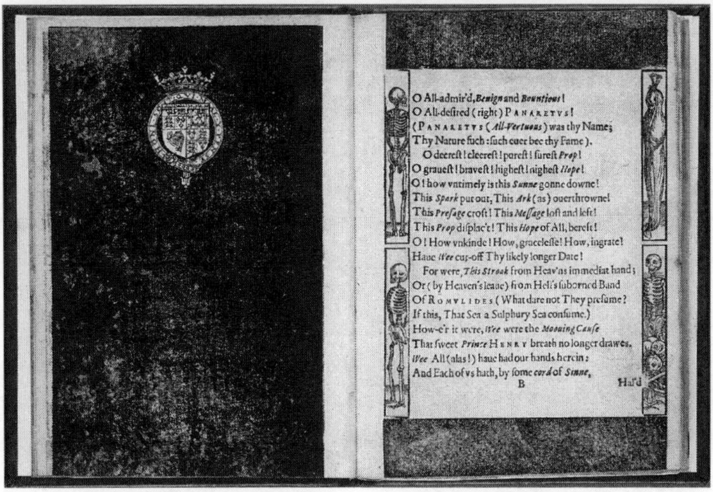

11. Opening from Joshua Sylvester, *Lachrymae Lachrymarum* (London: Humfrey Lownes, 1612). The text is printed on rectos only; versos are black mourning pages bearing Prince Henry's royal arms, gartered and crowned. The volume also had a black wrapper composed of an intaglio title page and end page.

tears are no use for the dead" (figure 11). At the same time the withdrawal of semantic meaning from the page makes us miss it. Positioning readers to welcome the return of words, however conventional or inadequate, black pages release an epistemophilic drive at the heart of grief that is the expression of a will to live, and perhaps therefore an intimation that comfort may be had. A kitchen servant in *Tristram Shandy* gives voice to this drive with admirable lack of inhibition when he learns of the death of Tristram's brother: "He is dead, said Obadiah—he is certainly dead!—So am not I, said the foolish scullion."

All the same, black pages profoundly disrupt our reading experience by bringing the outside in, hollowing out spaces, opening and closing off passageways within the text. John Quarles's *Regale lectum miseriae, or, A kingly bed of miserie in which is contained a dreame, with an elegie upon the martyrdome of Charles, late King of England, of blessed memory* (London: for Edward Crouch, 1649)

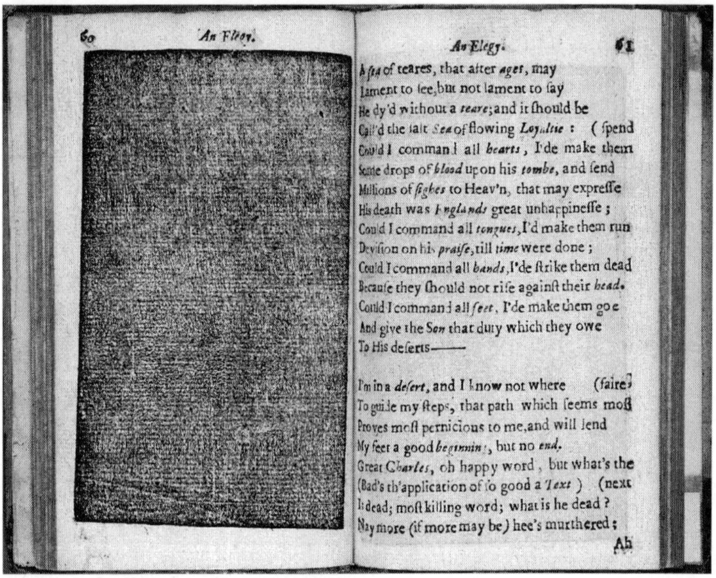

12. Opening from John Quarles's *Regale lectum miseriae, or, A kingly bed of miserie in which is contained a dreame, with an elegie upon the martyrdome of Charles, late King of England, of blessed* memory (London: for Edward Crouch, 1649). The "Elegie upon that never to be forgotten Charles I" has a separate title page, dated 1648, and the text is printed on rectos only; versos have one of four black intaglio wood-cut designs whose swirling white lines produce the effect of "mourning curtains"; the volume also had a black end page.

contains a series of black woodcuts with swirling white lines that represent what the Huntington Library catalogue calls "mourning curtains" (figure 12). The fright-effect suggested by these black plates is a product of the fact that they posit a space that is simultaneously void and impenetrable. Behind them is nothing, in architectural terms they would open onto a blank wall. Choosing their moment, acting on the very occasion when we seek comfort in reading, they tell us that writing attacks the surfaces of which it is a part, undermining the already impossible space that is the volume of a book.

Thoughts like these tormented Antonin Artaud, and one of Derrida's most sustained attempts to engage with the problem of the surface is to be found in the reading he conducted of the "*subjectile*," the strange word that others before him isolated as the symptom of Artaud's struggle with the materials of his art. "Subjectile" is a term that was almost nonextant when Artaud used it, three times, to describe his maddened sense that the surfaces on which he painted either *deadened* his expression or were hostile to and likely to betray it.[21] Although other painters had sometimes used the term more neutrally, to designate any treated surface that had been prepared to receive paint, in Artaud's writing "subjectile" always indicates that the thought of the surface has become insupportable. And in his essay of 1986 "Maddening the Subjectile" Derrida was quick to honor and elaborate Artaud's problem. He could do this, to a certain extent, from the perspective of his own sanity. For even if we take "subjectile" as simply as possible to mean the materials, as distinct from the forms and meanings, that comprise a painting, we are already in an unthinkable space, "between the beneath and the above," says Derrida, but actually in both places at once. For if the subjectile is the backing material of a painting through which you can't see or pass (for example, the canvas and successive layers of paint), it is *also* the surface through which it seems you can. Surface and substrate, screen and stretcher, the subjectile is everything that is transparent *and* everything that is opaque as you look at a painting; and if you imagine that you are an artist like Artaud, whose vocation is to forget his own long acquaintance with the rules of perspective, you can begin to understand the panic that contemplation of the subjectile might induce. A plate glass window that ends the flight of a bird and also a surface that withdraws if you lean on it, the subjectile will only let you down.

The difficulty of Derrida's essay on the subjectile derives in part from the protective generosity with which he has there bound his language to Artaud's, even as he follows his strange and volatile subject in resisting all relations of relation such as *being bound to* or *supported*. ("Not that language is just a support, as you might say of a textile, of a wall or a panel," Derrida begins, only to realize, immediately, that you might not say of a textile, of a wall, or of a panel that it is "just a support" (MS 160).)[22] But the problem of the surface attracted Derrida before and after this engagement, and away from the influence of Artaud he could sometimes view matters in a different light. In "Freud and the Scene of Writing" he describes with evident enjoyment the strange space produced by the layers of celluloid, paper and wax that comprise Freud's "mystic writing pad." "Let us note." he says,

> that the *depth* of the Mystic Pad is simultaneously a depth without bottom, an infinite allusion, and a perfectly superficial exteriority; a stratification of surfaces each of whose relation to itself, each of whose interior, is but the implication of another, similarly exposed surface. Like the psychic apparatus of which it is the model, the mystic writing pad is, at one and the same time, infinitely deep, and absolutely superficial. (*WD* 224)

This nest of layered surfaces recurs in *Archive Fever* (1995), when Derrida argues that the dedication written by Freud's father Jacob on the flyleaf of the family Bible that he had rebound for his son's thirty-fifth birthday also commemorates Sigmund's circumcision:

> The foliaceous stratification, the pellicular superimposition of these cutaneous marks seems to defy analysis . . . Each layer seems to gape slightly, as the lips of a wound, permitting glimpses of the abyssal possibility of another depth destined for archaeological excavation. To read, in this case, requires working . . . on substrates or under surfaces, old or new skins, the . . . epidermises of books or penises—and the very first figure recalls, at least figuratively, the circumcision of the father of psychoanalysis. (*AF* 22–23)

The rebound Bible takes its place among the various strata of skins and cuts that, according to Derrida, would be the Freudian archive in its impossible entirety. Trying to complicate the notion of a writing surface as something exterior and accessory to inscription, he reveals the abyss to be full of surfaces, one under the other, all the way down.

Two years later Derrida found himself looking back at these issues in "Paper or Me," a written interview first published in a French journal of media studies, where Marc Guillaume and

Daniel Bougnoux began their questions by invoking the typographical experiments Derrida had conducted in the 1970s and 1980s. "You have written books with various ways into them, with various formats, or folds, as if to elude the surface of the paper and the traditional linearity of writing," they reminded him. "You have clearly dreamed of making the page a theatrical scene (for the voice, but also for the body), of hollowing out a depth in it, and also often an abyss." And then they asked: "To what extent does paper already function as multimedia? To what extent has it been adequate for you to communicate your thinking" (*PM* 41)? Derrida's reply will appear extravagant only to those who have not learned to recognize the peculiarity of his thought whereby any one theme can be made to stand for all the rest:

> Seeing all these questions emerging on paper, I have the impression (the impression!—what a word, already) that I have never had any other *subject*: basically, paper, paper, paper. It could be demonstrated, with supporting documentation and quotations, "on paper": I have always written, and even spoken, *on* paper: on the subject of paper, on actual paper, and with paper in mind. Support, subject, surface, mark, trace, written mark, inscription, fold—these are themes that have gripped me with a tenacious certainty. (*PM* 41, translation modified)

To embrace a question in this manner is characteristic of Derrida. He will say he is never not talking about Freud; or that the destabilization of the status of "written-oral" has always been the "very element" of his work—you can see it is on the tip of his tongue to claim that everything he needs to say is already in the term "impression," the word he had recently used to organize his discussion of what he calls "the technical substrate" in *Archive Fever* (*AF* 25). Here he is also putting playful weight on the words "subject" and "support," knowing that a disquisition on either would entail the whole of his thought. But what is *paper* that it could emerge and find a place in this class of his singular obsessions?

The short answer is that we don't know. When we say "paper," Derrida writes, "are we naming the empirical body that bears this conventional name? Are we already resorting to a rhetorical figure? Or are we by the same token designating a 'quasi-transcendental paper,' whose function could be guaranteed by any other 'body' or 'surface,' provided that it shared some characteristics with 'paper' in the strict sense of the word (corporality, extension, the capacity to receive impressions, and so on?)" (*PM* 52)? The problem of knowing what paper is goes far beyond the fact that it can be made of various materials—we could resolve that problem by saying, as Derrida does, that our concern is with a more general "paper form of thinking," one that implies only *some* kind (even an electronic kind) of material "backing or support" for writing. But for Derrida the problem survives in the very terms we have just used to clear the matter up, for "backing" or "support" (such as a rhetorical figure might give to the expression of a thought) is precisely the concept for which we have no warrant. In short, we are back where we started in 1966, facing the "infinitely deep," "absolutely superficial," and entirely unmasterable space of the mystic writing pad (*WD* 224). Only now we are in a position to appreciate the consequence of the gesture by which, in that essay, Freud used paper to model thought, but used it, says Derrida, "as if he would like to put himself *beyond a paper principle*."

In 1997 Derrida left the topic with the remark that the question of the surface would finally involve 'generalized, formalized and deconstructive reflection on what will have been meant by *being-beneath*, the submission or subjected-ness of subjectivity in general.' But here's an alternative: what if we stopped thinking about the surface, stopped trying to think beyond paper, and worked instead to develop a model of writing whose structure was that of being-within, rather than being-on, a structure that would allow us the option of *doing without, rather than thinking beyond, a paper principle*.

Derrida's own arguments would enable the experiment. Responding to the questions posed to him by Guillaume and Bougnoux, he remarked that paper "has always been more than . . . the supposed neutrality of a support" for it "gets hold of us bodily . . . through every sense and through every fantasy." As an instrument of writing, paper performs as several media at once, participating in an operation that is spatial and temporal, visible, tangible and sonorous, active but also passive. Which means that paper does something other than simply *support* what must "be something other than" merely the *operation* of writing; maybe it can be described, says Derrida, as "the becoming-opus, or the archive, of operative work" (*PM* 42). And suddenly a new thought opens before us—that we will never have understood writing if we continue to think in layers, for "on" is only a special case of being "in" the world, a case that is locally stabilized but far from stable, and a fantasy more dominant than it should be, perhaps, since it prevents us from seeing that writing is dispersed, unsupported, through the depths of everything.

And here is the place to remark that there are, in fact, two types of subjectile in Derrida's essay on Artaud: one can be represented by the hard reflective surfaces of glass or steel, the other is porous and absorbent. Thinking about this second type, Derrida remarks: "We have to learn not to rush to seize, to understand, we should take the time needed to absorb the ink of so many words that should deposit themselves slowly in the thickness of the body: exactly the one of the subjectile whose nature we still do not understand" (MS 164). So we might say that if Artaud found the subjectile to be hateful, sticky, a demonic support within whose surface it was possible to drown, and if Derrida showed himself to be also susceptible to its uncanny effects, he was nevertheless receptive (what a word, already!) to an alternative that, after all, was better suited both to his ethics and to the radical patience of his reading method. Wood, fabric, canvas, or paper; think carefully and you will realize that the receptive surface is a membrane that changes and is changed by what it bears. "Your paper is damp, and the ink sinks through it," as one schoolboy says to another in Erasmus's *Familiar Colloquies*. Writing becomes part of the material that supports it—this, I think, is what we should make of Derrida's description of paper, or of any writing surface, as "the becoming-opus, or the archive, of operative work" (*PM* 42). And we should note what follows, for this is Derrida's last writing lesson to us: writing can never be *on* something without also being within, about, and in response to it. *What is writing on?* Writing is written on writing. Writing supports writing, all the way down. Soaked into its environment, unique but reactive and therefore never itself, writing draws from and gives back to the world, already changed in its untranslatable place.

Notes

INTRODUCTION

1. Terry Belanger, "Analytical Bibliography," in *Book Collecting: A Modern Guide*, ed. Jean Peters (New York: R. R. Bowker, 1977), 99–100. See W. W. Greg, "Bibliography—An Apologia," *The Library* 4th series, 13, no. 2 (1932): 113–43, which explains the consequence of bibliography as a textual science.

2. Peter M. McDonald has recently argued that literary theory and book history have more in common than is easily understood in the aftermath of the "theory wars" and that Derrida's work in particular "connects rather than separates theorists and book historians by pointing out their shared interest in radically re-thinking the idea of the book." Peter McDonald, "Ideas of the Book and Ideas of Literature: After Theory?" *PMLA* 212, no. 1 (2006): 223.

3. Jean-Luc Nancy, "Blank Opening," in *Reading Derrida's Of Grammatology*, ed. Sean Gaston and Ian Machlachlan (London: Continuum, 2011), 99. Derrida's writing is also radically *unpredictable.* He once said of himself: "it is to Heraclitus that I refer myself in the last analysis," an aphorism Nicholas Royle explains with reference to another, attributed to Heraclitus: "One cannot step twice into the same river, nor can one grasp any mortal substance in a stable condition, but it scatters and again gathers, it forms and dissolves, and approaches and departs." After reading Derrida, notes Royle, "it seems appropriate to suggest that one can't step *once* into the same river." Nicholas Royle, *After Derrida* (Manchester: Manchester University Press, 1995), 127.

4. As recorded by Benoit Peeters in *Derrrida: A Biography*, trans. Andrew Brown (London: Polity Press, 2013), 168. In 1980, at the delayed defense of his thesis at the Sorbonne, Derrida remembered this exchange and noted that "Recalling this reply today I am not sure that I understand it very well" (PTT 35).

5. Laurence Sterne, *The Life and Opinions of Tristram Shandy, Gentleman*, Book 1, Chapter 14.

6. As Alan Bass points out in his translator's introduction, Derrida explained in a footnote to the list of sources in *Writing and Difference* that these essays are not woven or "sewn" but "tacked" or "basted" together in the order of their publication, without the fine-tuning and hence the shape that hindsight could have given them (*WD* ix–xiv).

7. "There is a lot less meaning around than there is information. That's because all you need for information is reliable covariance . . . Information is ubiquitous but not robust; meaning is robust but not ubiquitous." Jerry Fodor, *A Theory of Content and Other Essays* (Cambridge: MIT Press, 1990), 93.

8. Madeleine David, *Le débat sur les écritures et l'hiéroglyphe aux XVIIe et XVIIIe siècles, et l'application de la notion de déchiffrement aux écritures mortes* (Paris: S.E.V.P.E.N., 1965); André Gourhan, *Le geste et la parole* (Paris: A. Michel, 1964–65); *L'écriture et la psychologie des peuples* (Paris: Armand Colin, 1963).

9. But see Gaston and Machlachlan, eds., *Reading Derrida's Of Grammatology*, a collection that offers an eclectic set of ways to understand the consequences of *Grammatology,* and issues a call for its re-translation (p. xxv).

10. Scribble (from the Latin *scribere*) suggests something hurriedly written or drawn whose production is disreputable (perhaps poetry or a novel) or a set of marks too idiosyncratic to be read. But Derrida's own interest in scribble primarily concerned the fact that it cannot be read aloud: if "grammatology" is speech about writing, "scribble" is writing about writing—as a title, it points to writing as a critical apparatus that "would not be excluded from its objects. And for us it would no longer be simply an object" (Sc 116).

11. "Grammatology must pursue and consolidate whatever in scientific practice has always already begun to exceed the logocentric closure. This is why there is no simple answer to the question of whether grammatology is a 'science.' In a word I would say that it *inscribes and delimits* science; it must freely and rigorously make the norms of science function

in its own writing; once again it *marks* and at the same time *loosens* the limit which closes classical scientificity" (*Po* 36).

12. See Freud, "Negation" (1925) (SE 14:235–39).

13. See David Farrell Krell, "All You Can't Eat: Derrida's Course, *Rhétorique Du Cannibalisme* (1990–1991)," *Research in Phenomenology* 36, no. 1 (2006): 130–80.

14. Martin Heidegger, *Introduction to Metaphysics*, trans. Gregory Fried and Richard Polt (New Haven: Yale University Press, 2000), 131.

15. Also in Lev. 19:10: "And thou shalt not glean thy vineyard, neither shalt thou gather every grape of thy vineyard: thou shalt leave them for the poor and the stranger: I am the Lord your God"; and Deut. 24:19: "When thou cuttest down the harvest in thy field, and hast forgotten a sheaf in they field, thou shalt not go again to fetch it: it shall be for the stranger, for the fatherless, and for the widow, that the Lord thy God may bless thee in all the work of thy hands."

16. See Sean Gaston, *Derrida, Literature and War: Absence and the Chance of Meeting* (London, Continuum, 2009), 73–74.

17. Gregory L. Ulmer, *Applied Grammatology: Post(e) Pedagogy from Jacques Derrida to Joseph Beuys* (Baltimore: Johns Hopkins University Press, 1985).

18. Ulmer, *Applied Grammatology*, 71.

19. Ulmer, *Applied Grammatology*, 18, xii.

20. Derrida gives a good description of this method of writing, which is also Jean Genet's, in *Glas*: "The text is spit out. And . . . saliva is the element that also glues the unities to one another. Association is a sort of gluing contiguity, never a process of reasoning or a symbolic appeal; the glue of chance [*aléa*] makes sense, and progress is rhythmed by *little jerks,* grippings and suctions, patchwork tackling [*placage*]—in every sense and direction—and gliding penetration" (142).

21. Ulmer, *Applied Grammatology*, 46; see also xi–xii, 18–30, 32–67.

22. But since the claim is now famous let's have a look at it in its context in *The Postcard*, where Derrida, addressing his lover, shows himself to be haunted, like the rest of us, by the desire for proximity: "Myself I am a man of speech, I have never had anything to write. When I have something to say I say it or say it to myself, *basta.* You are the only one to understand why it really was necessary that I write exactly the opposite, as concerns axiomatics, of what I desire, of what I know my desire to be, in other words you: living speech, presence itself, proximity, the proper, the guard, etc. I have necessarily written upside down" (*PC* 194).

23. See, for example, *G* 49a, 59–60a; and *PC* 159, 172, 178, 192.

24. All the same, Ulmer's project offered more than the "reversal of phoneticization" or the elevation of the "homophonic principle." He took from *Grammatology* a commitment to attend to writing in an expanded sense, as a cultural "scripting" that needed to be pursued in a variety of emergent media; and he used its name to designate what others have called media studies, "a new organization of cultural studies . . . a new mode of writing whose practice could bring the language and literature disciplines into a more responsive relationship with the era of communications technology in which we are living" (4). *Applied Grammatology,* which was published in 1985, is largely concerned with performance art and cinema, but its general commitment to forms of meaning that exceed or affront those of the voice were, like Derrida's own, prescient of the development of other new media and of the academic disciplines that would emerge to study them. Using the resources offered by the non-phonetic features of mathematical operations and visual artistic practice, Ulmer has contributed to this discipline in a series of monographs and essays that chart what he sees as a shift from literacy to "electracy," a phase of cultural development that he regards as being both older and younger, other and larger, than written literacy.

25. Jonathan Goldberg, *Writing Matter: From the Hands of the English Renaissance* (Stanford, CA: Stanford University Press, 1990).

26. Goldberg, *Writing Matter*, 7.

27. C. G. Jung, *The Collected works of C. G. Jung*, ed. Sir Herbert Read et al., trans. R. C. F. Hull et al. (New Jersey: Princeton University Press, 1970) vol. 16, par. 367.

28. Christopher Johnson, *System and Writing in the Philosophy of Jacques Derrida* (Cambridge: Cambridge University Press, 1993).

29. Michel Serres, *Hermes III, La Traduction* (Paris: Editions de Minuit, 1974), 17–21; quoted in Christopher Johnson, *System and Writing in the Philosophy of Jacques Derrida*, 3

30. Nicholas Royle, *Jacques Derrida* (London: Routledge, 2003), 4, 25.

31. As Derrida conceived it, psychoanalytic graphology is really just an alternative name for cultural graphology; the choice is left open because psychoanalysis would necessarily be deformed by the new understanding of writing that it would continue to inform: "psychoanalysis sees itself called to collaborate with a graphematics to come, rather than with a linguistics dominated by an old phonologism" (*WD* 220), says Derrida, already gearing up for the decisive critique of Lacan that he was to write in 1974.

32. I was helped here by Benoit Peeters's remarkable *Derrida: A Biography*.

33. For indispensible guide to Derrida's early intellectual environment see Edward Baring, *The Young Derrida and French Philosophy* (Cambridge: Cambridge University Press, 2011), especially chapters 6–8.

CHAPTER ONE

1. Walter Benjamin, "The Cultural History of Toys," in *Walter Benjamin: Selected Writings*, ed. Michael W. Jennings, Howard Eiland, and Gary Smith (Cambridge, MA: Harvard University Press, 2005), 115.

2. Geoffrey Bennington, *Interrupting Derrida* (London: Routledge, 2000), 95–103.

3. In a well-known interview with Derek Attridge, Derrida described the compulsive desire to write that began in his adolescence as "an obsessive desire to save in uninterrupted inscription, in the form of a memory, what happens—or fails to happen. What I should be tempted to denounce as a lure—i.e.: a totalization or gathering up—isn't this what keeps me going? . . . to reserve, perhaps encode, in short to render both accessible and inaccessible. And deep down this is still my most naïve desire" (TSI 34–35). The desire is naïve because inscription is precisely what interrupts, enables, and destroys by saving what happens.

4. In *The Psychopathology of Everyday Life* Freud gave a less exceptionable explanation: "When we come to mistakes in reading and writing, we find that our general approach and our observations in regard to mistakes in speaking hold good here too—not surprisingly, in view of the close kinship between these functions" (SE 6:106).

5. A typographical error in the English translation, which then reads "this did prevent Freud from posing the fundamental juridical problem of responsibility," has passed unobserved among some commentators on this passage. The French reads "ce qui ne l'a pas empêché de poser le problème juridique fondamental de la responsabilité, devant l'instance de la psychanalyse, par exemple à propos du *lapsus calami* meurtrier" (*WD* 290; *ED* 340).

6. Sebastiano Timpanaro, *The Freudian Slip: Psychoanalysis and Textual Criticism* (1974), trans. Kate Soper (London: Verso, 2010), passim.

7. For the difficulty of apportioning blame for shoddy print work see David Norton, *Textual History of the King James Bible* (Cambridge: Cambridge University Press, 2005), 54–55. Norton concludes that "because of the divided responsibility for errors, because they tell only part

of the story of the accuracy of the work, and because there is also fallibility in the present identification of them, one should not depend much on generalizations from errors." I will propose something beyond this—namely, that the difficulty in identifying errors is theoretical rather than practical, and admits no resolution.

8. "In healthy people, egoistic, jealous, and hostile feelings and impulsions, on which the pressure or moral education weighs heavily, make frequent use of the pathway provided by the parapraxes in order to find some expression. . . . Acquiescence in these parapraxes and chance actions is to a large extent equivalent to a compliant tolerance of the immoral. Among these suppressed impulses no small part is played by the various sexual currents" (SE 6:276).

9. "It may, in general, seem astonishing that the urge to tell the truth is so much stronger than is usually supposed" (SE 6:221).

10. Ernest Jones, "The Psychopathology of Everyday Life," *The American Journal of Psychology* 22, no. 4 (1911): 477–527, 503–4.

11. "Every time we make a slip in talking or writing we may infer that there has been a disturbance due to mental processes lying outside our intention: but it must be admitted that slips of the tongue and of the pen often obey the laws of resemblance, of indolence, or of the tendency to haste, without the disturbing element succeeding in imposing any part of its own character on the resulting mistake in speech or writing. It is the compliance of the linguistic material which alone makes the determining of the mistakes possible, and at the same time sets the limits up to which the determining can go" (SE 6:221–22).

12. André Green, "Psychoanalysis and Ordinary Modes of Thought" (1979), in *On Private Madness*, trans. Pamela Tyrell (London: Karnac, 2005), 18. Joyce MacDougal, who was Marguerite Derrida's training analyst, was also a pioneer in this area.

13. "In Lichtenberg's *Witzige und Satirische Einfalle* [Witty and Satirical Thoughts, 1853] we find this: 'He had read so much Homer that he always read "*Agamemnon*" instead of "*angenommen* [supposed]."' Here we have the whole theory of misreading" (SE 15:38–39).

14. Freud's position was that nothing in the psychical realm is unmotivated, or left to the purely physiological determinants of the brain. In this letter to Fliess he was quick to catch himself in the act of expressing an unconscious wish: "What I meant was some very big number, but that particular one emerged . . . you will . . . rightly expect that the unconscious had hastened to determine the number that was left open

by consciousness," and he decided that his unconscious had seized the opportunity to express his anxiety over his achievements, and satisfaction that the retirement of a rival meant that his career was at an end, "while I still have everything in front of me" (SE 6:242–43).

15. John Heydon, *A new method of Rosie Crucian physick* (London: Thomas Lock, 1658).

16. W. W. Greg, *A Companion to Arber* (Oxford: Clarendon Press, 1967), 294–98.

17. Archbishop George Abbott, one of the original translators of the King James Bible, testified that he remembered a time "when greater care was had about printeing, the Bibles especiallie, good compositors and the best correctors were gotten being grave and learned men, and the paper and letter rare and faire every way of the best," and he lamented that "now the paper is nought, the composers boyes, and the correctors unlearned." See David McKitterick, *A History of Cambridge University Press*, vol. 1 (Cambridge: Cambridge University Press), 197. McKitterick argues that the missing "not" was "almost certainly" the result of sabotage carried out as part of the struggle between Barker and other printers for control of the Bible patent. David Norton concurs, while leaving open the (surely unlikely) possibility that the omission could also have been a compositor's "jape." See Norton, *A Textual History of the King James Bible*, 95–96.

18. Johnson, *System and Writing in the Philosophy of Jacques Derrida*, 138.

CHAPTER TWO

1. Derrida argues that histories of writing that privilege phonetic systems and elements (and there have hitherto been no others) are the expression of an instrumentalism that sees writing as a technical extension of speech. Phoneticism is thus part of, and a powerful resource for, the habits of thought that constitute western metaphysics: "logocentric teleology (a pleonastic expression); opposition between nature and institution; play of differences between symbol, sign, image, etc., a naive concept of representation; an uncritical opposition between sensible and intelligible, between soul and body; an objectivist concept of the body proper and of the diversity of sensory functions (the 'five sense' considered as so many apparatuses at the disposition of the speaker or writer); opposition between analysis and synthesis, abstract and concrete . . . ; a concept of the concept upon which philosophical reflection has left little mark; a reference to consciousness and to the unconscious which

would necessarily invoke a more vigilant use of these notions and some consideration of those studies that make these notions their theme; a notion of the sign that philosophy, linguistics and semiology illuminate rarely and feebly" (*Grammatology* 82, translation modified).

2. Christopher Norris, *Derrida* (Cambridge, MA: Harvard University Press, 1988), 74. Derrida suggests both spacing and punctuation as sites where we might note the non-phonetic elements of our own alphabetical writing: "Now, if one ceases to limit oneself to the model of phonetic writing, which we privilege only by ethnocentrism, if we draw all the consequences from the fact that there is no purely phonetic writing (by reason of the necessary spacing of signs, punctuation, intervals, the differences indispensable for the functioning of the grapheme, etc.), then the entire phonologist or logocentrist logic . . . becomes narrow and superficial" (*Po* 23).

3. Lindley Murray, *English Grammar, adapted to the different classes of learners. With an Appendix, containing Rules and Observations for Promoting Perspicuity in Speaking and Writing* (Menston: Scolar Press, [1795] 1968), 159.

4. *Ben Jonson Volume 8: the Poems, the Prose Works*, ed. C. Herford, P. Simpson and E. Simpson (Oxford: Oxford University Press, 1947), 467 and 551.

5. Johnson, *System and Writing*, 89.

6. Hägglund, *Radical Atheism* (Stanford: Stanford University Press, 2008), 15.

7. Ibid., 18.

8. Ibid., 27.

9. Derrida's unease with what he is doing in these texts is expressed and deflected along the way in comments such as those voiced by one of the interlocutors in "Restitutions of the Truth in Pointing," who points out that the discourse is more organized than it pretends: "Your stanzas disappear more or less rapidly, simultaneously cut and interlaced, held together at the very crossing point of their interruptions. Caesuras that are only apparent, you won't deny it, and a purely faked multiplicity. Your periods remain without enumerable origin, without destination, but they have authority in common" (*TP* 261).

10. Barbara Johnson, translator's introduction to *Dissemination*, xxviii–xxix.

11. Stephane Mallarmé, "Un coup de dés jamais n'abolira le hasard," in *Oeuvres Completes*, ed. Henri Mondor and G. Jean Aubrey (Paris: Gallimard-Pléiade, 1945), 455.

12. In his long reading of Abraham and Torok's re-consideration of Freud's case of "The Wolf Man" Derrida expresses admiration for these two authors as being among the few critics and analysts who have understood that the power of the signifier resides in its fleeting and transmissible nature (F xxviii–xxix).

13. Visual poetry often gives readers the impression that it has survived from an earlier age: In the late sixteenth century Gabriel Harvey described the "newly-popular" shaped poems as "madd gugawes and crockchettes of late foolishly revised by sum," while Dick Higgins, poet, printer, and co-founder of Fluxus says of the six shaped poems that survive in *The Greek Anthology* from the Hellenistic period "one does not feel when one reads them as if they were innovative or avant-garde in their time. Rather, they seem like surviving texts from a lost tradition of some kind." Dick Higgins, *Pattern Poetry: A Guide to an Unknown Literature* (Albany: State University of New York Press, 1987), 14; Gabriel Gabriel Harvey, *Letter Book*; cited in Higgins, *Pattern Poetry*, 14. Derrida showed that he had thought about the long tradition of using mis-en-page to order commentaries on religious and other texts when he described his decision to juxtapose a discussion of Hegel's canonical philosophical writing with the "re-writing of a more or less outlaw, barely receivable writer-poet Genet" in *Glas*: "This contamination of a great philosophical discourse by a literary text that passes for scandalous . . . may seem violent—already in the 'page lay-out.' But it also re-joined or reawakened a very old tradition: that of a page that set out otherwise its blocks of texts, interpretations, interior margins" (*Pt* 349–50).

14. Roland Barthes, *Les Lettres Françaises* 1429 (29 March 1972), quoted in Benoit Peeters, *Derrida, A Biography* (London: Polity, 2013), 235. For a sympathetic account of the ways in which Derrida's writing informed Adami's drawings and vice versa, see Renée Riese Hubert, "Derrida, Dupin, Adami: 'Il faut être plusieurs pour écrire,'" *Yale French Studies* 84 (1994): 242–64. This fine essay speaks at times as if for Derrida's own aspirations to see his concepts pictured. The excuse of those who argue that Derrida used mis-en-page to make his concepts visible is that he sometimes relaxed his own critical vigilance in this regard. In "+R+," an essay that accompanies a set of Adami's drawings in the series of occasional papers put out by the Maeght gallery (*Derriere le miroir* 214 [May 1975], which is reproduced as part of *The Truth in Painting*), Derrida was scrupulously conscious that it is all too easy in writing about painting to frame oneself as a fool ("any discourse on it, beside it or above, always

strikes me as silly . . . and the more so when it is pertinent") (*TP* 155). He even says of the invitation to write about Adami's work that "making me speak, it was putting me in the wrong but it was too late and that will have taught me a lesson" (*TP* 157). But the essay still leaves even the most attentive reader with the impression that, in spite of his efforts to resist the temptation, Derrida has been lured into feeling, and even arguing, that he could *see* his own arguments in the drawings of his friend.

15. Charles Dickens, *The Mystery of Edwin Drood*, chap. 4.

16. Watching Heidegger make a similar move, and wondering whether it did not, after all, throw him back onto the ground of an "unperceived metaphysics," Derrida noted "I am merely defining a risk, I am not yet saying Heidegger runs it, simply, nor above all that one must in no circumstances run it: in wanting to avoid it at all costs, one can also be seen rushing towards the false exit, empirical chit-chat [or] spring-green impulsive avant-gardism" (*TP* 30).

17. Stanley Morison, "Venice and the Arabesque," in *Selected Essays of the History of Letter Forms in Manuscript and Print*, vol. 1, ed. David McKitterick (Cambridge: Cambridge University Press, 1981) 149–58.

18. Sir David Brewster, *The Kaleidoscope: Its History, Theory and Construction* (London: John Murray, [1819] 1858), 134; cited in Jonathan Crary, *Techniques of the Observer: On Vision and Modernity in the Nineteenth Century* (Cambridge, MA: MIT Press, 1992), 116.

19. In "Cartouches," an essay on the work of his friend Gérard Titus-Carmel, Derrida repeatedly promised, "later, elsewhere" to deal with the question of the crossing or interlace of the line but finally had to admit that he couldn't face it: "So many thongs, so many leashes. Too much to say here. I give up" (*TP* 193, 242).

20. Francis Meynell and Stanley Morison, "Printer's Flowers and Arabesques," *The Fleuron* 1 (1923): 1–46. In 1564 Henry Denham became the first English printer to use flowers in combination, and by 1566 their use in England was already widespread.

21. But it has been estimated that only about one in twenty late medieval books "had framing decorative work at one or more textual units." Kathleen Scott, "Design, Decoration and Illustration," in *Book Production and Publishing in England 1375–1475*, ed. Jeremy Griffiths and Derek Pearsall (Cambridge: Cambridge University Press, 1989), 31. Beyond Scott's essay, very little scholarly work has been undertaken either on the function or on the varied and shifting kinds and designs of illuminated borders in late medieval books.

22. B. H. Bronson, *Facets of the Enlightenment: Studies in English Literature and Its Contexts* (Berkeley: University of California Press, 1968), 356.

23. Henry R. Plomer, *English Printers' Ornaments* (London: Kegan Paul, Trench, Trubner and Co., 1916) 47–49; A. W. Pollard, *Early Illustrated Books: A History of the Decoration and Illustration of Books in the Fifteenth and Sixteenth Centuries* (London: Kegan Paul, Trench, Trubner and Co., 1918), which considers the development of printed ornaments as a process of the printer's "long emancipation from his long dependence on the help of the scribe" (35). See also Juliet Fleming, "How to Look at a Printed Flower," *Word and Image* 22, no. 2 (2006): 165–87; Juliet Fleming, "How Not to Look at a Printed Flower," *Journal of Medieval and Early Modern Studies* 38, no. 2 (2008): 345–71; and Juliet Fleming, "Changed Opinion as to Flowers" in *Renaissance Paratexts*, eds. Helen Smith and Louise Wilson (Cambridge: Cambridge University Press, 2011), 48–64.

24. Robert Bringhurst observes that printed type "gives the illusion of superhuman speed and stamina—and superhuman precision and patience—to the writing hand." *The Elements of Typographic Style* (Point Roberts, WA: Huntley and Marks, 2004), 19.

25. Dwiggins cited in D. B. Updike, *Printing Types: A Study in Survivals*, 3rd edition (Oxford: Oxford University Press, 1962) 106–7; Meynell and Morison, "Printer's Flowers and Arabesques," 3–4.

26. See Harold Bayley, *The Tragedy of Sir Francis Bacon* (New York: Haskell House, [1902] 1970), 49. "Figure 34, which appears at first sight to be merely a row of vases or urns will, on examination, be seen to consist of three, if not four, Rosicrucian symbols most cunningly packed together."

27. See Scott, *Design, Decoration and Illustration*, 64.

28. In the nineteenth century "branched" or foliated work, together with its geometric and calligraphic "variants," came under the intense scrutiny of Western orientalists, who, sidelining the presence of figural imagery in Islamic art, saw the "arabesque" as the fundamental expression, either of an "oriental spirit" that had a horror of empty space and a taste for abstraction or of a more specifically Islamic weltanschauung that responded to restrictions placed on figural representation by developing abstract modes of design expressive of a non-representable divine order. The name "arabesque" contains these conflicting meanings even as it collapses the chronological, regional, dynastic, and theological differences within the artistic practice it attempts to define, and

it is consequently of little use as an analytic term. I retain it here only to describe the re-invention, by sixteenth-century European artists, of abstract designs imported there from the Muslim world.

29. See Meynell and Morison, "Printer's Flowers and Arabesques," 8; and Alain Gruber et al., eds. *The History of Decorative Arts: The Renaissance and Mannerism in Europe*, trans. John Goodman (New York: Abbeville Press, 1994), 23–111 and 276–345.

30. E. Kuhnel, *The Arabesque: Meaning and Transformation of an Ornament*, trans. Richard Ettinghausen (Graz: Verlag für Sammler, [1949] 1976); quoted in Gruber, *The History of Decorative Arts,* 278.

31. For a comprehensive list of these books see Meynell and Morison, "Printer's Flowers and Arabesques," 11–15; also Gruber *The History of Decorative Arts* 34–35 and 284–298.

32. Kuhnel, *The Arabesque*; quoted in Gulru Necipoglu, *The Topakapi Scroll: Geometry and Ornament in Islamic Literature* (Santa Monica, CA: The Getty Center, 1995), 75. Necipoglu offers a compelling description of the ways in which, in the nineteenth century, "the so-called arabesque . . . was assigned a purely decorative function, that differed fundamentally from the iconographic tradition of Western representational art," suggesting that the arabesque's "alleged absence of meaning" facilitated its appropriation by Western industrial designers "in an age of eclecticism and revivalism" 62–63. Sixteenth-century Europe was, however, already such an age, and the gestures that "Westernized" the arabesque as a style devoid of meaningful purpose surely have their origins here, in a moment that, with the advent of print, was witnessing the first large-scale commodification of both Western art and alphabetic meaning.

33. Katharine F. Pantzer, "The Serpentine Progress of the STC Revision," *The Papers of the Bibliographical Society of America* 62 (1968): 308–309.

34. Rodolphe Gasché gives a fuller account of the same problem in *The Stelliferous Fold: Towards a Virtual Law of Literature's Self-Formation* (New York: Fordham University Press, 2011), 7–9. For a lively account of the origin of "textus," see John Schneid and Jesper Svenbro, *The Craft of Zeus: Myths of Weaving and Fabric* (Cambridge, MA: Harvard University Press, 1996).

35. Robert Scholes, *The Rise and Fall of English* (New Haven: Yale University Press, 1998), 74.

36. Richard Glazier, *A Manual of Historic Ornament* (Toronto: Dover, 2002), 168.

37. Elizabeth Gaskell, *Cranford* (London: Penguin, [1853] 1976), 125–26.

38. Richard Glazier, *Manual of Ornament*, 168.

39. Staging his feelings about this assignment, Derrida gives a good account of the energy it takes him to write when, for implacable theoretical reasons, he can never be done: "I give up. Discouragement. I'll never get to the end of it, I'll never be quits. I'll have to start again after treating as residues, more than once, all the words I've just used, I shall have to use a lot of them . . . put them in perspective, turn them round in all directions through a series of deviations, variations, modulations, anamorphoses. And then stop at a given moment (twenty pages more or less), in an apparently arbitrary fashion, as he did at the end of the year, more or less, in the mode of contingency" (*TP* 199–200).

40. An early use of the term "flower" that may not have been observed before occurs in a Bill of Complaint issued in 1598 to the Star Camber by the Draper Simon Stafford, explaining that the custom of the city made it lawful for him to print, with the result that he "did furnish himselfe to his very great Costes and Charges wth presse, cases, Chases frisketes composinge stickes, galleys, flowers, letters and all necessary implementes tooles and instrumentes meete and necessarye for the said Trade." Star Chamber, Eliz., S 7/22, transcribed in C. B. Judge, *Elizabethan Book-Pirates* (Cambridge, MA: Harvard University Press, 1934), 165–69. Otherwise the earliest known use of the term occurs in 1683, in Joseph Moxon, *Mechanick Exercises on the whole Art of Printing*, ed. H. Davis and H. Carter (London: Oxford University Press, 1962), 25–26, which remarks that a master printer "Provides also Flowers to set over the head of a Page at the beginning of a Book."

41. *The poesie of floured prayers. Containing sundrie meditations and prayers gathered out of the sacred letters and virtuous writers: disposed in the forme of the alphabet, of the most virtuous Lady, the Lady Elizabeths name. Set forth by John Conway* (London: T. Purfoot for Valentine Sims, 1611).

42. Which also means, perhaps, that it does not know what a text is. As Derrida said of *Glas*, his own florilegium, "What, in sum, is it all about? About citing, about reciting, the *genet* [the broom flower, a play on Genet's name] for pages at a time? About interpreting it, executing it like a piece [*morceau*] of music? . . . Not even an anthology. Some morsels [*morceaux*] of anthology. As an invitation, if possible, to rebind [*relier*], to reread [relire] . . . Nevertheless, these morsels cannot, naturally, be bound" (*TP* 118b).

43. For a clarifying reading of Derrida's account of the parergon in Kant's work see Jonathan D. Culler, *On Deconstruction* (Ithaca: Cornell University Press, 1982), 193–99.

CHAPTER THREE

1. Derrida often said that, even before his commitment to philosophy, his interest was in literature. But this interest took the form of some unresolvable philosophical questions, such as those he recalled in his 1980 thesis defense. "What is literature? And, first of all, what is it to write? How is it that writing can disturb the very question 'what is?' and even 'what does it mean?' To say this in other words . . . when and how does an inscription become literature, and what takes place when it does? To what and to whom is this due" (PTT 36).

2. The two essays may be found together in Jacques Lacan, *Écrits: The First Complete Edition in English*, trans. Bruce Fink (London: Norton, 2006). I have used two earlier translations: "The Agency of the Letter in the Unconscious, or Reason Since Freud," trans. Alan Sheridan in *Écrits: A Selection* (London, Tavistock, 1977), 138–168; and "The Seminar of the Purloined Letter," trans. Jeffrey Mehlman, *Yale French Studies* 48 (1973): 39–72. For a first-hand account of the personal and intellectual relations between Derrida and Lacan and their consequences for the development of psychoanalysis in France, see Elizabeth Roudinesco, "Lacan and Derrida in the History of Psychoanalysis," *European Journal of Psychoanalysis* 2 (1995–96); and Elizabeth Roudinesco, *Jacques Lacan and Co.: A History of Psychoanalysis in France, 1925–1985*, trans. Jeffrey Mehlman (Chicago: University of Chicago Press, 1990) 385–88.

3. Barbara Johnson, "The Frame of Reference: Poe, Lacan, Derrida," *Yale French Studies* 55/56 (1977): 457–505.

4. "A break from naïve semanticism and naïve psycho-biographicism, an elaboration of a logic of the signifier in its literal materiality and its syntactical formality, an appropriation of the problematic of *Beyond the Pleasure Principle*, these are the most general forms of what seems at first glance to be a legible advance on the part of the Seminar" (PT 45).

5. Johnson, "The Frame of Reference," 505.

6. Molière, *Don Giovanni*, Trans. Richard Wilbur (London, Harcourt, 2001), act 3, scene 5.

7. For an earlier discussion of this practice and its ramifications, see Juliet Fleming, afterword to "The Textuality of Reading in Early Modern England," special issue, *The Huntington Quarterly* 73, no. 3 (Fall 2010):

523–52; and the essays collected in "The Renaissance Collage," ed. Juliet Fleming, Adam Smyth and William Sherman, special volume, *The Journal of Medieval and Renaissance Studies* 45, no. 3 (2015).

8. Adam Smyth, "'Rend and teare in peeces': Textual Fragmentation in Seventeenth-Century England," *The Seventeenth Century* 19 (2004): 36–52.

9. In *Glas* and the *Truth in Painting* Derrida used the term "detaille" to describe the relation between "cut" and "size" in regard to the notion of the "colossal": "I have proposed to call the detail, or the detaille, the movement from cise, which is always small or measured, to the disproportion [la démesure] of the without-cise, the immense. The dimension of the effigy, the effigy itself, would have the fictional effect of demesuring. It would de-cise, liberate the excess of cise" (*TP* 121).

10. *Maison rustique, or The countrie farme. Complied in the french tongue by Charles Stevens amd Iohn Liebault, doctors of physicke. And translated into English by Richard Surflet, practioner in physicke* (London: Edmund Bollifant for Bonham Norton, 1600), 348–50.

11. For a good discussion of this art, see Hiram Manning, *Hiram Manning on Decoupage* (London: Dover, 1980); and Danielle O. Kisluk-Grosheide, "Cutting up Berchems, Watteaus, and Audrans: A *Lacca Povera* Secretary at the Metropolitan Museum of Art," *Metropolitan Museum Journal* 31 (1996) 81–97.

12. *Lettres de Mademoiselle Aissé a Madame Calandrini* (Paris: Édition Stock, 1943), 47; quoted in Kisluk-Grosheide, "Cutting up Berchems," 81.

13. *Mercure de France*, Dec. 1717, 2889–94, "Lettre écrite par M. Constantin a la Marquise de *** sur la nouvelle mode des Meubles en découpage"; quoted in Kisluk-Grosheide, "Cutting up Berchems," 94–97.

14. Hannah Woolley, *A Supplement to the Queen-Like Closet* (London: Richard Lownds, 1674), 70–71.

15. Woolley, *A Supplement*, 72.

16. Charles Dickens, *Great Expectations*, chap. 22.

CHAPTER FOUR

1. For an efficient description of what Derrida means by auto-affection see Forbes Morlock, "The Subject of Reading-3," in *Reading Derrida's Of Grammatology*, ed. Sean Gaston and Ian Maclachlan (London, Continuum, 2011), 124–26.

2. As Derrida testified in his delayed thesis defense, the aim of this abandoned project was to have been to bend, "more or less violently, the

techniques of transcendental phenomenology to the needs of elaborating a new theory of literature, of that very peculiar type of ideal object that is the literary object, a 'bound ideality' Husserl would have said." The limitation to Husserl's otherwise rigorous argument, as Derrida saw it, was that his ideal objects were predicated on a kind of "intuitionism, the absolute privilege of the living present," and that in ignoring the history of the constitution of these objects, transcendental phenomenology sought recourse in a language that also "remained naïve" about its own phenomenological enunciation (PTT 36–40).

3. See Donald McKenzie, *Bibliography and the Sociology of Texts* (Cambridge: Cambridge University Press, 1999); and Roger Chartier, *The Order of Books: Readers, Authors and Libraries in Europe Between the Fourteenth and the Eighteenth Centuries*, trans. Lydia G. Cochrane (Stanford: Stanford University Press, 1994). See also Roger Chartier, "Texts, Forms and Interpretations," in *On the Edge of the Cliff: History, Language and Practice* (Baltimore, Johns Hopkins University, 1997), 81–90.

4. Hannah Segal, *Yesterday, Today and Tomorrow*, ed. Nicola Abel-Hirsch (London: Routledge 2007), 54.

5. D. W. Winnicott, "Transitional Objects and Transitional Phenomena: A Study of the First Not-Me Possession," *International Journal of Psychoanalysis* 34 (1953): 89–97.

6. James Strachey, "Some Unconscious Factors in Reading," *International Journal of Psychoanalysis* 11 (1930): 323.

7. James Strachey, "Some Unconsious Factors," 324.

8. Benoit Peeters, *Jacques Derrida: A Biography* (London: Polity Press, 2013), 284.

9. D. W. Winnicott, "The Capacity to be Alone" (1958), in *The Maturational Processes and the Facilitating Environment: Studies in the Theory of Emotional Development* (London: Karnac Books, 1965), 30.

10. W. R. Bion *Intention and Interpretation* (London: Karnac Books, 1970), 12. Keats described negative capability as the capacity to be "in uncertainties, Mysteries, doubts, without any irritable reaching after fact and reason." Letter to George and Tom Keats, 21 December 1817, in *The Letters of J. Keats: 1814–1821*, edited by H. E. Rollins (Cambridge: Cambridge University Press, 1958), 193.

11. John Conway, *Meditations and praiers, gathered out of the sacred letters, and virtuous writers: disposed in the fourme of the alphabet of the queene majesties name. Whereunto are added comfortable consolations* (London: H[enry] Wykes,1569).

12. Biographies of Sir John Conway (1535–1603), assumed to be the author of this work, record that he was interrogated and possibly imprisoned in 1583 in connection with the Somerville-Arden case. The *Dictionary of National Biography* suggests that it was "probably in connection" with Conway's putative imprisonment over this case that he wrote *Meditations and Prayers*, but by then the work had already gone through four editions. Daniel Starza Smith (*John Donne and the Conway Papers* [Oxford: Oxford University Press, 2014], 36) notes that Sir John Conway "should not be confused with any of the John Conways of Rhuddlan and Bohryddan, Flintshire, distant Welsh kinsmen," and it may be that the customary ascription of *Meditations and Prayers* to Sir John is such a mistake. The Conways of Flintshire were an old Anglo-Welsh family, later known for their recusant leanings: among them the John Conway who sat for Wales in Elizabeth's first parliament from 1562–67, and died in 1578, is the most likely candidate to have been the author of *Meditations and Prayers*.

13. Robert Bringhurst, *The Elements of Typographic Style* (Point Roberts, WA: Hartley and Marks, 2004), 138. This inlaid or recessed effect is sufficiently consequential that when the eighteenth century British printer John Baskerville wanted to give his work a more modern look he had his printed sheets ironed to remove their sculptural edges.

14. Stephane Mallarmé, "Un Coup de Dés jamais n'abolira le hazard," in *Oeuvres Completes*, ed. Henri Moder and G. Jean Aubrey (Paris: Gallimard, 1945), 455.

15. Gilles Deleuze and Félix Guattari, *A Thousand Plateaus: Capitalism and Schizophrenia*, trans. Brian Massumi (London: Continuum, 2004), 187.

16. Thomas Middleton, *The Blacke Booke* (London: Thomas Creede for Jeffrey Chorlton, 1604).

17. Ibid., A4r.

18. Ibid., F3v.

19. See William Jackson, "Printed Wrappers of the Fifteenth to the Eighteenth Centuries," *Harvard Library Bulletin* 6, no. 3 (1952): 313–21.

20. These titles have not been collected before. They include John Taylor, *Great Britaine all in blacke for the incomparable losse of Henry, our late worthy Prince* (London: Edward Allde for I. Wright, 1612); George Chapman, *An Epicede or funeral song on the most disastrous death of . . . Prince Henry* (London: Thomas Snodham for John Budge, 1612); Richard Niccols, *The three sisters teares shed at the late solemn funerals of the royal deceased Henry* (London: Thomas Snodham for Richard Redmer,

1613); a collection of poems by Tourneur, Webster and Heywood published under the combined title *Three Elegies on the most lamented death of Prince Henry* (London: Nicholas Oakes and Felix Kingston for William Welbie, 1613) and also issued in separate parts; and Joshua Sylvester, *Lachrymae Lachrymarum* (London: Humfrey Lownes, 1612); Christopher Brookes's *Two Elegies consecrated to the neuer-dying memorie of . . . Henry Prince of Wales* (London: Thomas Snodham for Richard More, 1612); John Taylor, *The Muses Mourning: or funeral sonnets on the death of John Moray Esquire* (London: s.n., 1615); *The Lieutenant of the Tower his Speech and Repentance*, (London: G. Eld for N. Butter, 1615); Patrick Hannay, *Two Elegies, on the death of our soueraigne Queene Anne* (London: Nicholas Oakes, 1619); and John Taylor, *A Living Sadness, in duty consecrated to the memory of . . . James, King of Great Britaine* (London: E. Allde for H. Gosson, 1625). The final page of the anonymous *Funerals of the High and Mighty Prince Henry,* printed by Thomas Snodham in 1613, shows heavy ink smudging, which suggests it may once have had a black wrapper.

21. As Derrida records, in 1932 Artaud described "a bad drawing in which what is called the subjectile has betrayed me"; fifteen years later he complains about the unresponsiveness of the page at which he "could probe, cut, scrape, file, sew, unsew, shred, slash, and stitch without the subjectile ever complaining" (MS 154, 160).

22. For an excellent reading of Derrida's essay that makes this point, see Herman Rapaport, *Later Derrida: Reading the Recent Work* (London: Routledge, 2003), 121–136.

Index

Adami, Valerio, 59–60, 96, 151n14
"A" pages, 66, 68, 132–34
arabesque, 69–70, 153n28, 154n32
arche-writing. *See* writing
archive, 28, 36–37, 39, 55–56, 62, 99, 105–11, 113, 123, 138
archive fever. *See* archive
Artaud, Antonin, 17, 136–38, 141, 160n21
Aufhebung, 108–9
auto-affection, 113–14
auto-immunity. *See* auto-affection

Barker, Robert, 47–48
Bayley, Harold, 66
beauty, 79–83
Benjamin, Walter, 32, 63, 96
Bennington, Geoffrey, 32–33
Bible, 44–45, 47–48, 127, 138; Exodus, 48; Ezekiel, 17, 18; John, 100–101; Leviticus, 19, 145n15; Numbers, 17
Bible patent, 48, 149n17
bibliography, 1–2, 5, 9, 18, 61–62, 115
biblos, 2, 128–29
biolology, 26
Bion, Wilfred, 122
black pages, 28, 130–36, 159n20
black wrappers. *See* black pages
blank, 57, 60–61, 130–32
book history, 2–3, 9, 16, 23, 26–27, 32, 38–39, 61–62, 63, 98–111, 115, 128, 143n2
Bougnoux, Daniel, 139–40
Brewster, David, 63
Bringhurst, Robert, 129

calligraphy, 59
Caputo, John, 95
castration, 42, 96–97
chance, 92–93
Chartier, Roger, 115
chiasmus, 59
circumcision, 96–97, 138
clinamen, 94
Cohen, Marcel, 10
combinatorial systems, 26
context, 6, 27, 34–35, 38, 93–94, 101
Conway, John, 75–78, 80–81, 123–27, 159n12
counterproduction, 40

cultural graphology, 1–2, 14–18, 20–26, 28, 32, 36, 39, 62, 87, 93, 114, 117, 123
cutting, 28, 35, 83–84, 87, 94–111, 157n9
cybernetics, 26

damask ware, 69
David, Madeleine V., 10
deconstruction, 7, 12, 15, 16, 20, 21, 28, 33–35, 55, 58, 62, 95, 140
découpage, 109–11, 132
Deleuze, Gilles, 130
Derrida, Jacques: as author, 5, 145n22, 147n3, 150n9, 151n13, 151n14, 155n39; as book historian, 2–3, 6; composition of his works, 5–6, 10, 29, 30; on Freud, 4, 6, 28, 32–33, 36, 37, 50, 139–40; legacy, 2; in 1967, 3, 6, 12, 14, 17, 26, 35, 37, 113; on Rousseau, 5, 9, 33–34; translation of his works, 7, 8, 11, 20; wordplay, 21–22
Derrida, Jacques, works of: "Aphorism Countertime," 4; *Archive Fever*, 4, 11, 17, 37, 96, 138–39; *Cinders*, 56–57; "Circumfession," 95; *Deconstruction in a Nutshell*, 95; *Dissemination*, 4, 22–23, 56–58, 93–94, 95, 96; "Freud and the Scene of Writing," 15, 35–36, 38, 46, 48, 54–55, 95, 122, 138, 140; *Glas*, 17, 18, 20, 21, 56–57, 59, 60, 71, 72, 75, 84, 86, 95, 96–97, 104, 105, 106–9, 111, 151n13; 155n42; *Grammatology*, 3, 5–6, 7, 8, 10, 11, 12, 13, 14, 15, 18, 20, 22, 24, 27–30, 32, 33, 51–52, 54, 56, 70, 82, 91, 93, 98, 112–15, 117; "Heidegger's Ear," 18; "Living On," 57; "Maddening the Subjectile," 137–38, 141; *Margins of Philosophy*, 57, 130; "Mes Chances," 4, 48–49, 71, 92–94; *On Touching*, 4, 71; *Paper Machine*, 11, 12, 17, 128, 138–41; *Points*, 5, 71; *Positions*, 3, 32; *The Postcard*, 17, 21; "Punctuations," 157n2; "Purveyor of Truth," 88–91; *Resistances of Psychoanalysis*, 33, 91, 95; "The Rhetoric of Cannibalism," 18; "Scribble (Writing Power)," 11; "This Strange Institution Called Literature," 120; *The Truth in Painting*, 8, 17, 20, 28, 46–47, 57, 59–60, 62, 63, 72, 73, 79, 82–83, 95, 96, 97, 107, 157n9; *Voice and Phenomenon*, 6; "What Is a Relevant Translation?," 37; *Writing and Difference*, 5, 6, 10, 13, 15, 16–17, 20, 29, 33, 36, 37, 38, 58, 71, 112, 115
Derrida, Marguerite, 29, 114, 117, 122
destinerrance, 3–4
detail, 96–97, 105, 110–11, 157n9
Dickens, Charles, 60, 111
différance, 3, 6, 7, 8, 15, 26, 28, 54–55, 91, 95
dissemination, 35, 59, 72
divisibility, 28, 91–95

Eckersley, Richard, 56
emblems, 102–5
entamer, 8
environment mother, 122, 129
Erasmus, Desiderius, 141
errata lists, 47
Estienne, Charles, 105–7

fabric, 70–73, 137
Fleurian, Dominique de, 56
flowers, 65, 70, 73–82. *See also* type ornament
fold, 57–58, 60. *See also* re-mark
framing, 63, 72–83, 94, 111. *See also* parergon
Freud, Sigmund, 14, 16, 44–45, 49–50, 87, 96, 119, 138; *Beyond the Pleasure Principle*, 33, 50; *The Interpretation*

of Dreams, 34, 47, 53–54; *Introductory Lectures on Psychoanalysis*, 39–44; *Note upon the Mystic Writing Pad*, 36, 138; *The Psychopathology of Everyday Life*, 16, 41–47, 49–50, 91–92, 147n4; 147n7, 148n11, 148n14

Gaskell, Elizabeth, 72–73
Genet, Jean, 18, 75, 96–97, 104, 107–8
Gibson, Sir John, 101–5
Glazier, Richard, 73
gleaning, 18
Goldberg, Jonathan, 24–25
grafting, 93–94, 97–101
grammar, 10, 11, 99
grammatology, 1, 7, 8, 10, 12–14, 17, 20, 24, 26, 51, 144n11; impossibility of, 12–14, 29; as a regional science, 13–14
graphematics. *See* Hjelmslev, Louis
Green, André, 29, 45–46, 122
Guattari, Félix, 130
Guillaume, Marc, 138, 140

Hägglund, Martin, 55–56
handwriting, 25, 52–53, 57, 98, 101–5, 128
Hegel, Georg Wilhelm Friedrich, 97, 107–8
Heidegger, Martin, 7, 18–19, 92, 95, 152n16
Henry, Prince of Wales, 134–35
hieroglyphics, 53–54
Hjelmslev, Louis, 14
human sciences, 27
Husserl, Edmund, 11, 157n23
hybrid books, 98–111

idealism, 23–24
information, 8–9, 23, 26, 32, 36, 99, 144n7
inhibition, 85, 116, 120–21
inscription, 8, 24, 58
intaglio wood cutting, 131
integrated wrappers, 132–34
iterability, 117

Johnson, Barbara, 57–58, 86, 89
Johnson, Christopher, 26, 49, 53–54
Jones, Ernest, 44–45, 47
Jonson, Ben, 52
Jung, Carl, 25

kaleidoscope, 63
Kandinsky, Wassily, 59
Kant, Immanuel, 79–83, 113–14
Klein, Melanie, 16–17, 18, 28, 29, 85, 88, 112–22, 124–25
Kristeva, Julia, 29

Lacan, Jacques, 29, 86–95, 118, 156n4
lace, 70–73
lapsus calami. *See* pen slips
Leroi-Gourhan, André, 10
letter, 23, 28, 48, 65–66, 86–94, 107, 115, 117–18, 129
Levi-Strauss, Claude, 9, 13
Life and Adventures of Tristram Shandy, The (Laurence Sterne), 4, 130–31, 135
literacy, 25
literality, 5, 16, 22, 28, 86–94
literary. *See* literature
literary criticism, 23, 27, 30, 106–7
literature, 5, 11, 16, 18, 22, 28, 29–30, 86–94, 101–5, 111, 120, 122, 156n1, 157n2
logocentrism, 13, 15, 18, 21, 22–24, 58
Lucretius, 92–95

Mallarmé, Stéphane, 22–23, 56–61, 84, 130
manuscript. *See* handwriting

mark, 93–94. *See also* trace
Mary Stuart, 99–100
materiality, 23–24, 50, 56–62, 88–94, 112–15, 118, 137–8
McDougall, Joyce, 122
McKenzie, Donald Francis, 115
Meynell, Francis, 65–66
micrography, 59
Middleton, Thomas, 131–32
misprints, 40–41
Molière (Jean-Baptiste Poquelin), 89–90
Morison, Stanley, 55–56
mourning curtains, 136. *See also* black pages
mourning wrappers. *See* black pages
Murray, Lindley, 52

Nancy, Jean-Luc, 3–4, 71
negative capability, 122, 158n10
non-phonetic writing. *See* writing
Norris, Christopher, 52

object relations, 17, 112–16, 119–23

page, 64–65, 130–32
paleography, 25
Pantzer, Katherine, 70
paper, 12, 28, 37, 58, 65, 127, 129, 139–42
parapraxes, 37, 39–40, 42–46, 50, 92, 148n8
parergon, 54, 73, 79, 82–83, 94. *See also* framing
part object, 114–15, 122
pen slips, 16, 28, 32, 35, 37–50, 147n5, 147n7, 148n11
philosophy, 7, 24, 38, 52, 86, 109, 111, 149n1, 156n1
phonetic writing. *See* writing
phonocentrism, 10, 38, 51, 90, 149n1
Poe, Edgar Allen, 86–89, 92–93
Ponge, Francis, 78–79
presentiment, 3–5, 9
preservation. *See* archive
print, 28, 39–40, 45, 64–85, 98–111, 129–36
printed errors, 28, 40–42, 44–45, 47, 49–50
printers' devil, 41, 49
printers' flowers, 70, 73. *See also* type ornament
printers' lace, 69–70. *See also* type ornament
proofreading, 40–41, 120
pruning, 99–101
psychoanalysis, 14, 16, 18, 29, 32–36, 86–93, 97, 112–23
psychoanalytic graphology, 16, 28, 29, 112–42, 146n31
punctuation, 52

Quintilian, 70–71

reading, 18–19, 27, 57–62, 84–85, 97–111, 120–23
remains, 105, 107–11
re-mark, 65, 85, 94. *See also* fold
reparation, 125–27
responsibility, 16, 35, 38–44, 120

Saussure, Ferdinand de, 9, 32, 91
Scholes, Robert, 70
science, 13, 15, 20, 26, 27, 52, 144n11
scribble, 144n10
Segal, Hannah, 116
semiosis, 8, 23
Serres, Michel, 26
sewing, 71–72, 107–11, 144n6
Shakespeare, William, 4, 92
signature, 22, 27, 104–5
sign-cutting. *See* sign-tailoring
sign-sewing. *See* sign-tailoring
sign-tailoring, 97, 107–11
skeleton frames, 75, 78, 126–27

Smyth, Adam, 101–2
Sollers, Philippe, 96
spacing, 7, 28, 52–62, 73, 91, 150n2
speech, 8, 9–19, 22, 24, 37, 51–53, 58, 71, 89–91, 149n1
Spivak, Gayatri, 7, 8, 10, 11–12, 20, 26, 29
Sterne, Laurence, 4, 130–31, 135
Strachey, James, 120–22
structuralism, 10
subjectile, 137–38, 141, 160n21
sublimation, 116–17
substrate, 61, 127–42
supplement, 6, 7, 34, 54
support, 8, 126, 127–42
surface. *See* support

technology, 27, 36
temporalization, 55–56
Timpanaro, Sebastiano, 39–40
Titus-Carmel, Gérard, 73
trace, 6–7, 8, 10, 15, 17, 47, 54, 55–56, 71–72, 93–94, 112–14. *See also* mark
transitional object, 119–20
translation, 37
type ornament, 28, 52–85, 155n40
typographical errors. *See* pen slips
typography, 56–66, 78, 126–27

Ulmer, Gregory, 20–21, 24, 146n24

vinet, 66–67, 70. *See also* type ornament
Voice. *See* speech

weaving, 70–72, 119
Weber, Ruth, 125
Wedekind, Frank, 49–50
Wicked Bible, the, 44–45, 47–48
Winnicott, D. W., 119–20, 122, 126, 129
Wittgenstein, Ludwig, 22
Woolley, Hannah, 109–10
word play, 21–24, 40
writing, 5, 8, 9, 10, 11, 16–17, 26, 28, 31–32, 46, 49, 51–54, 70, 112–15, 120, 123, 141–42, 156n1; arche-writing, 9, 17, 36, 54, 55, 56, 93, 97, 112; beyond the book, 2; as cutting, 97–111; Derrida's commitment to, 2, 6, 11–12; dislike of, 42, 116–18; and ethnocentrism, 24; history of, 16, 18, 21, 24, 28; ideographic, 21; instruments of, 16–17, 114–15, 126, 128, 140–41; in the expanded sense, 8, 15, 24, 26–28, 32, 36, 54, 56; in the narrow sense, 8, 9, 10, 15, 24, 26–27, 36, 59, 113, 115; metaphors for, 71–79, 119, 129; non-phonetic, 28, 51–54, 62, 70; phonetic, 16, 20–21, 51–54; psychopathology of, 16, 28, 32, 45–46, 116–19; science of, 9, 12–15; sociality of, 39; and speech, 89–91, 139; supports for 126–42; visual aspects of, 21–22, 54, 56–60, 65–68, 84–85, 129–30, 151n13, 151n14; as what happens, 9, 54. *See also* pen slips